Getting into

Psychology Courses

MPW Guides

Titles in this series

Getting into

Psychology Courses

Maya Waterstone

8th edition

Getting into Psychology Courses

This 8th edition published in 2010 by Trotman Publishing an imprint of
Crimson Publishing, Westminster House, Kew Road, Richmond,
Surrey TW9 2ND

Author: Maya Waterstone

© Trotman Publishing 2008, 2010
© Trotman & Co Ltd 1994, 1996, 1999, 2002, 2004, 2006

7th edn published in 2008 by Trotman Publishing
6th edn published by Trotman & Co Ltd in 2006 by James Burnett and
Maya Waterstone
5th edn published by Trotman & Co Ltd in 2004 as *Getting into
Psychology* by James Burnett and Maya Waterstone
4th–1st edns published by Trotman & Co Ltd in 2002, 1999, 1996 and
1994 as *Getting into Psychology* by MPW

British Library Cataloguing in Publication Data
A catalogue record for this book is available from the British Library

ISBN: 978–1–84455–226–9

Typeset by IDSUK (DataConnection) Ltd

Printed and bound in the UK by TJ International Ltd, Padstow, Cornwall

Contents

About the author

Maya Waterstone is a Director of Studies and careers adviser at Mander Portman Woodward (MPW) London. She is a qualified child and adolescent counsellor. She has also written articles for a religious studies magazine and is a teacher of religious studies at both GCSE and A level.

■ Acknowledgements

I am grateful for the help provided by Trotman Publishing, who allowed us to bring the information that we had prepared over a number of years for MPW students to a wider readership, and to those who worked on the earlier editions. Thank you also to the British Psychological Society, whose excellent website and range of publications made the job of writing this guide much easier, and to UCAS. I would also like to thank the admissions staff at the universities who provided the information on courses in Chapter 7 and John Meeske and James Burnett for their contributions to this book.

Maya Waterstone
January 2010

> For up-to-date information on psychology courses go to www.mpw.co.uk/getintopsych

About this book

Deciding what to study after A levels is a daunting task. There are already numerous books, guides and leaflets available to help you make your choice. So, why bother to write yet another? *Getting into Psychology Courses* is, as the title suggests, specifically for people wanting to do psychology at degree level. We hope it provides a clear and concise introduction to a subject which relatively few students do at school. It contains information on entry requirements, the length and content of the various courses on offer, and a little about the actual university psychology departments. It also provides some guidelines on making your UCAS application, writing your Personal Statement and preparing for an interview. If, after reading the following chapters, your decisions have been eased in any way, we will have achieved our goal.

This book is intended to complement, not replace, existing publications, many of which are included in the reading list at the end of the guide. Details of entry requirements, courses, campus facilities, etc. are constantly changing and, although the details in this guide are correct at the time of going to press, it is essential to check with UCAS and/or particular universities if you have any queries.

> For up-to-date information on psychology courses go to www.mpw. co.uk/getintopsych

Introduction

For 2008 entry, around 15,500 applicants applied for just under 14,000 places on psychology courses at UK universities. Psychology continues to be a very popular degree course option because it offers a number of well-defined career paths as well as being perceived by employers in general as being a valuable qualification, as it combines scientific analysis, mathematical skills and the requirement to be able to write coherent and structured essays.

Although there is not quite the pressure on psychology degree course places as there is for potential medics or vets, the application statistics show that applicants are certainly not guaranteed a place. Furthermore, many applicants have very clear ideas about which universities they wish to target (some of the most popular universities have up to 20 applications for every place) and so applicants need to think carefully about the strategies they are going to adopt in order to maximise their chances. This is why we have written this book: to give prospective psychology students advice about making a successful and convincing application.

Psychology: a popular subject

Psychology is an incredibly popular, increasingly competitive course of study at university. Its popularity is fuelled in part by the growing demand for psychologists across a wide range of workplaces. Students love studying psychology because it is eye opening, scientifically rigorous and readily applicable to life. Students are given the tools that allow them to see human relations and human behaviour through a special kind of lens, one that aims to give legitimate, evidence-based explanations for behaviour, rather than explanations based on common sense, proverbs or other metaphors. It is said that we are all 'naive psychologists' in that we all have our own explanations for various human behaviours. The trained psychologist, however, typically has three predominant qualities: a natural empathy, a strong background in scientific and statistical methods, and a drive to improve his/her own understanding that persists across a lifetime.

▉ More than meets the eye: the story behind how people act

Psychologists endeavour to explain behaviour, and no explanation is ever simple. Consider the case of eating disorders, where a person's eating habits (over-eating, under-eating or some other abnormal eating behaviour) are detrimental to their health and may be fatal if not corrected. How do we explain this?

One piece of the puzzle may be genetics – those biological characteristics we inherit from our parents. Anorexia nervosa, for example, may have a relatively strong genetic component, given that identical twins who share the disorder are more common than fraternal twins who share it. The brain structure known as the hypothalamus may also play a part in eating disorders, given that if you damage part of it in a rat, it may cause the rat to over-eat spectacularly or to starve itself to death. Furthermore, high levels of the neurotransmitter serotonin are linked to several problems such as vomiting, suppressed appetite, obsessions, phobias and anxiety – all of which feature somewhere in the broad range of eating disorders.

However, many of these physiological contributors seem to be beyond the control of the individual. Are people who suffer from eating disorders entirely at the mercy of their biological circumstances? Some research-ers have pointed out that the way we think can have a profound impact on our behaviour, sometimes even leading us to take action entirely against our healthy interests. People with bulimia nervosa, for example, may have an overly rigid thinking style, causing them to see the world in terms of black or white categories. When they over-eat, they may see it as a total catastrophe rather than a minor mishap and this compels them to rectify the mistake by purging. Similarly, a problem with estimating body sizes may lead to under-eating or purge behaviour. Some people with anorexia have difficulty making mental calculations of their own and others' body sizes.

And finally, is it important to consider the wider context of the individual with an eating disorder? Does their family background and upbringing play a part? Anorexia statistics are skewed in the direction of middle-class teenage girls. What might make them more vulnerable than other people? Research supports the idea that families of eating-disordered girls have more negative family interactions than other families. The psychodynamic tradition of psychology might argue that unresolved and unspoken con-flict existing within a family may spill over onto a vulnerable child, who then develops abnormal eating habits as a coping mechanism.

> With all the good research attempting to explain an important issue such as eating disorders, how are we to decide which, if any, is cor-rect? The psychologist understands that there are many things that affect human behaviour and sees each of the various explanations as valuable contributions to a complex puzzle.

■ Psychology experiments: can a person be evil?

Landmark experiments in the 1950s and 1960s banished forever the notion that evil acts could only be committed by evil people. Up until then, people committing outrageous crimes against other people were seen to possess some form of moral or character defect. While it is true that there are a number of dispositional (internal) factors linked to criminal behaviour, what these famous studies showed was that even an ordinary, everyday person could be manipulated into committing an evil act through social influences. Take Stanley Milgram's experiment conducted at Yale University in 1963, for example. By engineering a tightly controlled situation where partici-pants felt compelled to obey the supervising researcher who was with them, Milgram was able to induce normal, temperate men into electro-shocking another man to death. Only a select few refused the orders of the researcher and abandoned the experiment. Fortunately, in this case, the man who had supposedly died was a confederate of the experiment, who was only acting. The participants could not see him but rather, heard his cries from the adjacent room and believed in the reality of the situation.

Milgram identified a number of powerful social factors such as uncertainty, agentic shift and graduated commitment that, if harnessed, could be used to manipulate people into behaving in ways that they would never normally behave. He finishes his summary of the experiment with a thought-provoking question. If he was able to influence a group of normal, healthy men to commit such acts of violence against their fellow men, how much more would a government, with its infinitely greater power and resources, be able to influence society? Milgram had given us a profound insight into the nature of atrocities such as the Holocaust.

Many other studies since then have confirmed the awesome power of social influences in directing our behaviour. One that stands out is Philip Zimbardo's prison study at Stanford University. A group of students were recruited to take part in a simulated prison. They were randomly assigned to take the role of either a prisoner or a guard and placed in an area of the university that had been modified to look like a prison. One of the most striking elements of this study was how quickly the people involved took to their respective roles. The simulation was supposed to last for two weeks but had to be abandoned after only six days, as people conformed so strongly to their roles. Prisoners became stressed, dejected and began to lose a sense of themselves, while several guards became more and more tyrannical in their behaviour. Even Zimbardo himself, who had taken the title of Prison Warden, began to lose himself in the role.

> Studying psychology will open the doors to a deeper understanding of human behaviour. When we are called upon to explain another person's evil act, many of us might say: 'he is just a bad person.' A student of psychology will pose the question: 'What else might be going on?'

▪ Taking a scientific approach: a way to explain human behaviour

Problems with sleep are on the increase. It seems that nowadays every other person has trouble dropping off to sleep or waking early. Similarly, every other person seems to have an explanation and a cure for sleep problems. One interesting possibility involves the layout and structure of the bedroom. If, for example, there is a pointy edge, maybe from a door, cupboard, desk or ceiling rafter, aimed in the direction of the bed (known as a poison arrow), it is important to neutralise it in order to improve the quality of sleep that bedroom can offer.

How are we to determine which, if any, of the myriad explanations for sleep disturbance has validity? Do we have to go through them one by one, all the while suffering with poor sleep, until we find something that works?

Scientific methods, when applied to psychological issues, provide us with a powerful way of determining those explanations that are valid and those that should be confined to the realms of 'folk' psychology – interesting ideas that lack any true power.

The placebo effect, for example, is one anomaly that can point us in the right direction. This effect shows the power of belief to heal; a person given a sugar-pill (medically ineffective) who believes it to be actual medication can recover more rapidly from illness. This shows us that any treatment for a psychological problem must demonstrate its effectiveness over a placebo, or else the treatment is no better than wishful thinking. We can do this by dividing a sample of people with the illness into two groups and treating half with the placebo and half with the actual treatment.

In light of this, we can surely separate out explanations for sleep problems into two categories: explanations that have been subjected to a controlled experiment like the one described above, or explanations that have come about anecdotally from someone who has had a single experience and is passionate about the result. These single case studies can be compelling, but they tell us little about the true effectiveness of a particular explanation.

> When it comes to explaining psychological difficulties that you or your friends and family face, do we rely on single cases that we have heard or read about for our explanations, or do we seek explanations that are backed up by good, solid scientific research demonstrating their validity as an explanation? What are the dangers of relying on single case studies?

■ Making a real difference to people's lives

Imagine yourself sitting in front of a psychotherapist for the first time. Having struggled for some time with constant self-criticism, depression and intense anxiety that seems to come from nowhere (always at the most inconvenient times), you have finally summoned the courage to ask for help. If this were early last century, the therapist would most likely have been psychoanalytic, taking his lead from psychoanalytic pioneers like Sigmund Freud. Under that approach, your current struggles would be explained as the result of unresolved conflicts residing deep within your unconscious. Since these conflicts are not open to your awareness, it would be the therapist's job help bring those issues to your awareness, perhaps through hypnosis, dream interpretation or free association, so that you can understand them and 'work them through'.

Despite the literature containing numerous rich case studies illustrating the effectiveness of the psychoanalytic approach, it can sometimes struggle to hold up under scientific scrutiny of the sort described in the previous section.

Without taking issue with that approach, modern psychological treatments, or 'talk-therapies', have developed over the last 30–40 years, which focus on present, conscious thoughts, and have begun what is amounting to a revolution in the field of mental health. Aaron Beck, inventor of cognitive behaviour therapy (CBT), shows us that our immediate thought patterns cause us to interpret the world in systematic ways, sometimes ensnaring us in a tangle of negative or self-defeating thoughts. In comparison to traditional psychoanalytic approaches, which can take many years to unravel a person's neuroses, CBT is quick, effective and targets our illogical or dysfunctional thoughts from day one.

It is easy to see the power of this approach in a simple example. Imagine not receiving an important and expected call from your partner at a particular time. This event may lead to the thought: 'something is wrong'. In a short time, you may imagine worst-case scenarios, provoking massive anxiety, or question the motives of your partner, provoking an angry reaction. The cognitive approach would aim to test the validity of automatic thoughts, replacing them with more rational alternatives. The negative emotions would quickly be reduced or even extinguished as you pondered more reasonable alternatives.

CBT has repeatedly demonstrated its effectiveness in controlled studies and is at least as effective as antidepressant drugs for mild to moderate depression. This is just one area of psychology that not only stands up to scientific scrutiny but also has a profoundly positive impact on the human race as a whole.

Whether or not certain forms of psychotherapy can be backed up by evidence of their effectiveness, the goal is still the same and that is to help people deal with the struggles they face in life. Psychotherapy is personality change. This means that even when we have a powerful tool for personality change like CBT, we still need a wise, empathetic person to employ that tool. To paraphrase Samuel Butler, 'A man convinced against their will is of the same opinion still.'

What is psychology really like to study?

Psychology, the study of people and how they act and think, is an increasingly popular subject of study with over 100 higher education institutions offering degree-level courses in the subject either as freestanding degree programmes in their own right or as modules in other combined programmes. Despite this growth in student places, there are still, however, some popular misconceptions about the content of degree programmes. They do not offer students the chance to spend three years studying the works of Freud. Nor do they enable you to see into other people's innermost thoughts.

On the contrary, psychology is taught as a scientific subject and students spend most of their time studying the results of research into human behaviour and the theories which are based on experimental findings. The aim of this introductory chapter is to give you an insight into some of the typical psychological research findings you are likely to study in the course of a degree programme. For more information about psychology as a career, you should look at the British Psychological Society's (BPS) website: www.bps.org.uk.

In Chapter 2 we will look into the variety of psychology courses available at degree level.

Why is psychology so popular?

Overall, then, why is psychology such a popular subject for a first degree? There are several reasons.

- Potential students are attracted to a subject that gives them insights into human behaviour and most students of psychology have a basic interest in people.
- It is a particularly attractive subject for mature students who may already have touched on the subject during previous training. Business managers, nurses and social services staff may well have been introduced to some of the basic concepts of psychology and want to learn more.
- Psychology is a subject that can be seen to span both arts and science subjects. It attracts students who have broadly based interests and abilities, who do not want to be seen as either an 'arts' or a 'science' person.

Finally, although the subject of psychology has been studied at university level for a century – the first professor of psychology was appointed in 1919 – it is still seen as a comparatively 'new' subject and, because of the volume of research carried out around the world, students will be studying a subject in which the boundaries of knowledge are constantly changing. What is more, as a result of the diverse applications of psychology in, for example, healthcare, sports psychology and organisational development, many new and exciting work opportunities are being created.

Careers in psychology

Your career after a psychology degree

There are essentially three main career routes for those who complete a degree course in psychology.

1| To train as a professional psychologist by completing several years of further study and training at postgraduate level.
2| To enter work or postgraduate training which builds on or relates to knowledge gained during a psychology degree programme.
3| To find a graduate-level career which is unrelated to psychology but which may reflect your particular skills and interests.

The three routes are outlined in more detail below to give you an idea of what you might expect after three or four years of study.

According to Prospects, the UK's official graduate careers website, approximately 61% of psychology students who graduated from university in 2005 had found employment within 6 months of graduating. About 24% of 2005's graduates were undertaking further study (or combining study with work). The relatively high figure of psychology graduates continuing with their studies is an indication of the need to gain further qualifications in order to practise as a psychologist. For graduates going directly into employment, there was a wide range of destinations, including finance, clerical and office work, managerial positions and teaching.

Professional psychology

Fewer graduates than you might expect follow this route. In order to qualify as a professional psychologist your degree course must give you the Graduate Basis for Chartered Membership (GBC) of the BPS. This is normally gained by following a course that is accredited by the Society. Once they meet that condition, graduates will then have to start on a sometimes lengthy period of postgraduate study and practical experience to qualify for Chartered Status to enable them to practise professionally. The main professional career routes are described below.

9

Clinical psychology

This is the largest specialism in professional psychology. Working mainly in the National Health Service, clinical psychologists work with clients of all ages by assessing their needs, providing therapy and carrying out research into the effects of different therapeutic methods. Their clients may be otherwise normal people who may have one of a range of problems such as drug dependency, emotional and interpersonal problems or particular learning difficulties. The clinical psychologist's role should not be confused with that of the psychiatrist.

Entry to training programmes is highly competitive and you will need a good pass in your degree as well as relevant work experience. This can be of two kinds – either work experience in some aspect of clinical care or community work, or experience as a psychology assistant working alongside existing clinical psychologists in a health authority. Vacancies for assistants occur quite frequently, but after working in this role there is no guarantee of gaining entry to a professional training programme, which takes a further three years and leads to a Doctoral degree. This final stage of professional training can take the form of either full-time study at a university coupled with practical experience or an in-service training programme with a health authority.

Occupational psychology

In comparison with other professional groups, occupational psychologists can work for a variety of employers and can be employed in a number of different roles. In government departments such as the Department for Children, Schools and Families (DCSF) and the Ministry of Defence, psychologists can be involved in research or advisory work on the most effective ways of selecting, training and employing personnel. In the disability service they assess individual clients and advise on the kind of work and training which might suit them.

By contrast, in business consultancies, psychologists could be involved in the development of new psychological tests or in the design and delivery of company training programmes on topics such as teambuilding. In large companies, occupational psychologists might introduce new systems for staff training and development, while in applied research they could find themselves working alongside engineers on the design of the interface between equipment and its potential users. In short, there are many potential areas of employment and freelance work. To qualify for Chartered Status in this field, psychology graduates need to complete a specialist postgraduate course lasting one year and in addition have three years' supervised work experience. Further details are available from the BPS's website.

Educational psychology

Educational psychologists are experts in child and adolescent development. They work mainly for local education authorities and liaise with teachers and parents in identifying and assessing pupils and students with particular learning difficulties. These can range from dyslexia to disruptive classroom behaviour. Educational psychologists may not be concerned with the treatment of individual problems, but will act in a diagnostic, advisory and consultative role. The referral of children with special educational needs to special schools is a typical example of a situation in which an educational psychologist's advice would be sought. To qualify for this specialism requires a lengthy period of further study, training and experience.

Different arrangements apply in Scotland, where educational psychologists do not need teaching experience, but in England and Wales psychology graduates are required to complete a one-year course of teacher training and have two years' teaching experience before starting a postgraduate course in educational psychology. This is then followed by one year of supervised practice, making it the longest qualification period of any psychology specialism.

Forensic psychology

Often known as criminological psychologists, those in this professional group work mainly in the prison service, assessing prisoners in terms of their rehabilitation needs and also in terms of their level of risk. The assessment is usually based on psychometric test results and clinical interviews. In addition, forensic psychologists carry out research and put in place treatment programmes to change offending behaviour and often work with groups of offenders to achieve this aim. Some psychologists in this grouping may also appear in court proceedings to give an expert view on, for instance, the mental state of defendants.

Once again, the qualification period is three years and this comprises study for a postgraduate master's programme, recognised by the BPS, along with supervised work experience. For details, see the BPS website (www.bps.org.uk).

Health psychology

Health psychologists look at the links between healthcare and illness. This can include behaviour which carries with it a health risk (such as smoking or drug use); preventative measures (exercise, diet, health checks); the delivery of healthcare; and the psychological aspects of illness, such as how patients cope with pain or terminal illness. There are a number of accredited MSc courses for candidates who have achieved the GBC. Following this, candidates must gain two years' experience in a related field before being assessed by the BPS.

Sports psychology

Sports psychology is a growing field. Increasingly, professional sports-men and women are using psychologists to help them to improve their performances. Many football clubs, for instance, now employ sports psychologists to work with their players on an individual and team basis. The aim of the sports psychologist is to enhance performance by improv-ing the focus or the motivation of the participants, and to encourage a 'will to win'.

There are no specific qualifications necessary to go into sports psychol-ogy, other than the need for a psychology degree. Further information can be obtained from the British Association of Sport and Exercise Sciences, whose address is at the end of this book.

Counselling psychology

A counselling psychologist helps people to deal with problems. Typically, these might include bereavement or relationship and family problems. The counselling psychologist usually works on a one-to-one basis with the subject and tries to help them to develop strategies to deal with life problems. To attain chartered status as a counselling psychologist, an accredited postgraduate course or a BPS diploma is required following the GBC.

Psychologists in lecturing and research

Academic staff in universities and colleges of higher education will com-bine teaching activities, such as delivering lectures and running seminars and tutorials, with a commitment to carrying out research. Their task is to keep up to date with the latest research findings in their particular area of expertise. They will spend a considerable amount of time making applications for research funding and, once the research is completed, writing journal articles to publish their findings. Entry to academic posts in psychology is very competitive. Lecturers in higher education are not required to have a teaching qualification but those applying for lecturing posts will be expected to have a PhD and to have some published research. Lecturing posts in psychology may also arise in colleges of further education. For psychology graduates who want to teach in schools the situation is problematic because the subject is not part of the National Curriculum. On balance, it is easier for graduates to gain a place on a one-year certificate course to teach at primary level, but even here different course centres will have their own views about whether to admit psychology graduates, who will need to prove that they have the academic interests and experience to equip them for the role of primary teacher.

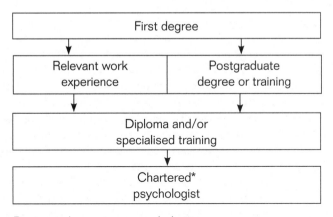

Routes to becoming a psychologist

*See page 9 for how to become a chartered psychologist

Other psychology roles

It is important to distinguish between the role of the psychologist and other professionals carrying out related work.

- **Psychiatrist.** A medically trained doctor who chooses to specialise in mental health by taking the membership examinations of the Royal College of Psychiatry. As a consequence of their medical training, psychiatrists can prescribe drug treatments. They will often work as part of a team with clinical psychologists.
- **Psychotherapist.** Works with both individuals and groups to provide long-term therapy. They will often encourage clients to reflect on their past experience and early development. In theory, a graduate of any subject can become a psychotherapist by taking a lengthy training programme of supervised clinical practice and seminars and, in addition, undergoing personal therapy themselves.
- **Psychoanalyst.** Bases his or her work on Freudian theory and tries to unearth the influence of the unconscious on clients' behaviour. Psychoanalysts work with individual clients in private practice rather than in paid employment. As with psychotherapy, the training period of at least four years includes the process of personal analysis.

Case Study

Alex chose to study psychology at degree level because he wanted a degree that would give him a choice of jobs after graduation. He did not study psychology at A level. Coming from an arts and humanities background (he studied history, politics and English literature at A level, and AS philosophy), he was surprised at the scientific content of his degree course in the first year.

'I suppose that my research into the courses I applied for was sketchy, to say the least. Of course, I read the prospectuses and was able to talk about the courses at interview, but I didn't look into the detail too closely. In fact, it was not really a problem since I had good GCSE grades in the sciences and mathematics, and they gave us lots of help on the course. At school, my friends who studied mathematics always complained about statistics, and when I realised that I would have to do this as part of my degree course I was horrified! When we covered statistics on the course, though, it was relatively easy. It was similar with the biological content – learning biology at school was not very interesting because it all seemed unconnected with my other subjects, but making links between the functions of, say, the nervous system, and theories about how we think and learn made it much more relevant.'

Related careers

There are several occupations for which a first degree in psychology is a useful entry qualification because of the particular knowledge or skills it provides. For example, an understanding of individual behaviour and social development is highly relevant to careers in teaching and social work. The study of statistical methods and the analysis and interpretation of statistical results can be useful in social and market research, especially when examining the results of large-scale surveys. Any insights psychology students gain into the nature of individual ability and aptitudes, and the ways these can be measured, will provide a foundation for a career in the assessment and selection of personnel. Knowledge you may acquire about physiological and cognitive psychology can be applied in ergonomics, or human factors design, as it is sometimes called. Yet again, an interest in other people's behaviour or personality may well provide the basis of careers which require an element of counselling or interpersonal helping.

By looking carefully at the content of degree programmes, the research interests of lecturing staff and specialist module options which might be available, you will soon begin to see if the course is pointing its students towards a particular career direction in applied psychology.

Options unrelated to psychology

Many graduates in psychology will choose not to apply the knowledge they have gained from their degree course, but instead, will use the skills they have gained in a wide range of other graduate-level careers. Approximately 40% of all graduate job vacancies in the UK are open to graduates irrespective of their degree subject. With a degree in psychology, therefore, it is quite possible to train as an accountant or a solicitor, enter general management, become a journalist or work in information technology. Much will depend on your particular interests and the skills you have developed. In studying psychology, students are often surprised by the number of different skills they develop and which they can use in their work after graduating:

- **information-seeking and research skills:** the ability to search databases and employ experimental methods
- **analytical skills:** the ability to think critically and weigh the evidence from different research findings
- **numeracy:** the ability to interpret statistical data and to assess the reliability of experimental results
- **IT skills:** the ability to use software packages for data analysis and psychological measurement.

These are in addition to the skills that most higher education students will acquire, such as the written communication skills developed in essay and report writing or the verbal communication skills used in group projects or seminar discussions and making presentations. As you can see, a psychology degree programme may help you to develop a broad range of skills which you can apply in the workplace, but you may need to make this apparent to potential employers.

■ Student views

'I chose to study psychology because of its dependence on scientific research. I like the idea that the subject is constantly changing and being updated. At UCL, we are expected to keep up to date with current issues and the results of new research. I think my strength in mathematics has been a definite advantage to me when looking at research methods. I would have struggled without A level mathematics.'

Manraj

'My initial idea, when choosing psychology as a degree subject, was to have a career as a psychologist (although to be honest I had not really researched this very thoroughly). We have lots of help with careers choices at the university, and I now think that I will use my degree as a 'general' degree and try to find a job with a city bank. Although it might seem strange, psychology will be an excellent basis for this because of the need to constantly analyse information.'

Steven

'I chose Birmingham because it has a very large psychology department and I thought that this would give me the chance to look at all aspects of psychology. I also wanted to study at a university with a campus feel but that was in the centre of a city. I have chosen to do my research project on forensic psychology and I think that this is what I would like to do as a future career.'

Emma

'Unlike a lot of other people on my course, I did not study psychology at A level. I knew that I might be at a disadvantage with my application because I would find it harder to justify my choice to an interviewer. My teachers at my college advised me to try to get some related work experience in order to strengthen my application.

I worked as a volunteer in a psychiatric ward in my local hospital once a week, and I also spent time in my holidays helping children with learning difficulties. Before my interviews I did as much research as I could on the related areas of psychology. It obviously worked because I received four offers!'

Peter

Case Study

Qian Qian's parents wanted her to study economics at university so that she could work in business or finance once she returned to China, but she enjoyed AS Psychology so much, she persuaded them to let her follow a Joint Honours degree in Psychology and Management. 'My parents are OK about this because I will still get a degree that is business related, and I persuaded them that psychology will help me to stand out from other students and will also be very useful in running a business. I was lucky not only because they agreed to this, but also because my school allowed me to study psychology at AS level. Chinese students I met socially, who went to other schools and colleges in the UK, were not given this choice.'

'I started the psychology course at Newcastle determined to be open minded about which area of psychology I would eventually specialise in. I am now in my third year and I have considered a lot of options but I have now decided that I will do a PhD in Clinical Psychology. Eventually, I want to work in a hospital environment but I want to go deeper into the subject before doing so. When I first started the course I had not expected it to be so demanding – I think that my idea about psychology was linked to what I had read about dreams and relationships, whereas in reality it is about scientific

*research and methods. I had to work hard in my first year to get up
to the necessary levels of understanding, but after that it all slotted
into place and I loved it.'*

Gemma

*'Having lived in China for 16 years I witnessed how people ignore
psychological problems. Those with mental illness are treated with
medicine which does not help their mental problems and the stigma
attached to needing psychological treatment prevents them from
seeking help from psychologists. Moreover, psychological treatments
are unavailable in some undeveloped countries. The apparently
inadequate provision in China has stimulated my interest further and
it has made me determined to pursue a psychology-related career,
possibly as a clinical psychologist.'*

Sally

03 Degree programmes in psychology

When choosing a degree course in psychology there are several points to bear in mind. Firstly, degree programmes will vary in their emphasis. Some will offer a general but comprehensive grounding in the subject. Others will tend to specialise in one branch of psychology. Secondly, admission to courses is usually open to students irrespective of the AS or A level subjects or other qualifications they have studied. However, some courses, which lead to a Bachelor of Science (BSc) degree in Psychology, may favour students with science subjects, because of the scientific or experimental nature of the degree course and the ancillary or minor subjects you may be expected to take.

Degree programmes leading to a Bachelor of Arts (BA) degree may look favourably at applicants with arts A level subjects. The distinction between the two is an important one, because the titles of the awards may reflect differences not only in main course content but also in the choice of subsidiary courses you can take. Those studying for science-based courses may have option choices in neuroscience or physiology whereas those on arts-based programmes may have options in social or developmental psychology.

General or specialised?

Not all first degree programmes in psychology have the same aims. Some are intended to be general in nature, giving a broad and comprehensive overview of all aspects of psychology. Others, by contrast, will attempt to give a special emphasis to one aspect of the subject. You will soon see from the course listings which follow whether a course has a general or specific emphasis. Examples of specialised courses include applied psychology, experimental psychology, occupational psychology and social psychology. There can be some benefits in completing this kind of degree, particularly if you already know that this aspect of psychology interests you. On graduation, it may also enable you to gain advanced recognition by the relevant professional group or division of the BPS.

Single subject, joint or modular?

Most university departments of psychology will offer a Single Honours degree in the subject, which means that your principal subject is psychology but that you may have to study other minor subjects in addition, which carry less weight in terms of marks and assessment. In addition, there are numerous examples of Joint Honours degrees in which you study psychology and one other subject to the same level. Examples include psychology and management, psychology and mathematics, psychology and sociology. This kind of programme enables you to study two subjects in depth, but you may need to check whether the overall workload is slightly higher than when studying for a Single Honours degree.

By contrast, modular degrees offer a range of different subject modules often linked by a unifying theme. Often called 'combined degrees', they are typically provided by institutes and colleges of higher education and enable students to study psychology alongside other subjects in the social sciences or humanities. With joint degrees, and combined degrees in particular, it is important for applicants to check to see if the degree course is recognised by the BPS and gives the GBC. Without this, it will be difficult to qualify professionally. The BPS's website provides an online search for accredited degree courses. The address is given at the back of the book.

Full time or sandwich?

Most degree courses in psychology are full time and last for three years, but some last four years, particularly those in Scotland, where it takes four years to gain an Honours degree. A small number of programmes, called sandwich courses, give students the chance to spend their third year on practical placements in companies or with different psychological services or agencies. Students then return to their university for their final year of study.

Although sandwich courses last four years, they can provide students with a valuable opportunity to gain first-hand experience which helps them not only to develop new skills but also to make decisions about which career path to take when they graduate. In one or two instances courses have a 'year abroad' option and arrange for students to spend a year studying at a university outside the UK, in Europe or North America for example.

Degree course content

Most degree courses offer a broad-based introduction to the subject to allow for the fact that many students will not have studied psychology before. This will be followed by increasing specialisation and advanced study as the programme progresses.

First year

In the first year you will be offered introductory courses in different aspects of psychology as well as in research methods, statistics and the use of information technology. You will hear about some of the key debates in the field of psychological research. For example, how far is human behaviour learned or inherited?

Second year

Courses in the second year will build on and extend subjects studied in the first year. You may also have to complete a series of laboratory or experimental classes to give you a practical insight into psychological research methods. The results of your second year assessment may well count towards your final degree result.

Third/final year

In the final year of a degree programme, students usually have the opportunity to choose modules or options that interest them, options which typically reflect the research interests of the staff in the psychology department concerned. At the same time, students will invariably undertake a major dissertation based on a research project of their own choosing. This is a significant piece of work and the choice of topic may well have some direct relevance to a student's future career choice. A typical course programme might consist of:

- **1st year:** methods and approaches to psychology; experimental psychology; statistical methods; social psychology; memory
- **2nd year:** research methods; further experimental psychology; behavioural psychology; cognitive psychology; developmental psychology
- **3rd year:** research project; option topics.

Definitions

For potential students who have not studied psychology before, the following definitions may be helpful in knowing what might be covered in different course modules.

- Cognitive psychology covers the relationship between the brain and human behaviour. It includes the study of memory, thinking and problem solving.
- Clinical and abnormal psychology concerns the symptoms, classification and theories of different forms of mental illness.
- Developmental psychology is the study of the process of human growth and development from birth to adulthood.

- Neuropsychology looks at the way the central nervous system operates in relation to the sensory processes – seeing and hearing, in particular.
- Psycholinguistics involves the interface between psychology and language, its acquisition and structure.
- Psychometrics is the measurement of attributes such as aptitude or personality, using psychological tests.

If you want to find out more, you can read one of the introductory text-books designed for first-year undergraduates. As well as the topics listed above you may find that a first degree in psychology will also cover some or all of the following:

- individual differences and psychological testing
- language acquisition
- social psychology
- statistics and experimental methods.

Entry grades

As with other degree subjects, the grades required for entry to degree courses in psychology vary from one university to another. Typically, the older-established universities may ask for 300–340 points, or a grade equivalent (BBB to AAB). By contrast, some of the newer universities may have slightly lower entry requirements. Given the statistical component of most degree courses, admissions tutors will also expect applicants to have a reasonable pass grade in GCSE Mathematics. Further details about the grades required by different universities can be found in some of the university and college listings (page 45).

Choosing a university

With over 100 universities offering psychology and psychology-related courses, how do you narrow down your choice to the maximum of five allowed on the UCAS form?

Things to consider:

- the grades that you are likely to achieve: there is no point in apply-ing to universities whose standard offers are significantly higher than the grades that you are predicted, or get
- the location of the university
- the facilities
- the course.

Turn to Chapter 7 for details of psychology courses at institutions across the UK.

You might also find it helpful to look at the league tables compiled by the national newspapers. Whilst all league tables should be used as a guide rather than as the definitive ranking of the university, they can be useful as a starting point if you are unsure how to start looking. The *Guardian's* university guide (http://education.guardian.co.uk/universityguide) allows you to look at the rankings of all UK universities, or you can narrow this down to just those offering your chosen subject. In its 2010 rankings of institutions offering psychology courses, the *Guardian* placed Oxford first, followed by UCL, St Andrews, then Royal Holloway. The ranking is based on a number of scores, including the government's teaching inspection score, an entry score based on grades achieved by students joining the courses, staff:student ratio, job prospects and spending. The *Guardian's* website allows you to re-order the tables to reflect your own criteria, or to change the weighting of the individual categories, For example, a ranking based on entry score places Oxford first, followed by Bath, UCL, then St Andrews. A ranking based on job prospects, on the other hand, has UCL in first place, followed by Oxford, Kent, then Royal Holloway.

04 The UCAS application

The UCAS Apply form

When you apply for UK universities, you do so using the UCAS system. The online UCAS form is accessed through the UCAS website (www.ucas.com). You register online either through your school or college, or as a private individual. Some of the information that you provide on the form is factual, such as where you live, where you have studied, what academic qualifications you have, details of examinations that you are going to take, and which university courses you are applying for. The final section on the form is the Personal Statement, where you write about why you want to study psychology, and about yourself.

Once your form is complete, it is then accessed by the person who will write your reference, who then checks it, adds the reference and then sends it to UCAS. After that, you can keep track of the responses from the universities with the online Track facility.

Planning your application

You need to prepare for your application well in advance. A possible timescale might look like this:

Year 12

May/June: Discuss your university options with your teachers, family, friends – as many people as possible. Book Open Days. Arrange work experience.

June/July: Make a shortlist of universities and courses.

August: Work experience. Research courses in more detail either on the university websites or by ordering prospectuses.

Year 13

September: Complete your application and send it off to UCAS – it will be accepted from 1 September onwards.

15 October: Deadline for applying for places at Oxford or Cambridge.

---

15 January: Deadline for submitting your applications to UCAS. They will consider late applications, but your chances are limited since some of the places will have already gone.

February–April: Interviews may be held.

March: If you have been rejected by all of your choices, you can enter UCAS Extra, a scheme that allows you to apply to other universities. See the UCAS website (www.ucas.com) for details.

April: Decisions will begin to go directly to the candidates. You will be given a deadline from UCAS to make your final decision around this time. You can choose **one** place as your Firm choice, and another (normally with a lower grade offer) as your Insurance place.

Summer: Sit your exams and wait for the results.

Results day: If you got the grades, congratulations! UCAS will send you confirmation of your place. If you missed your grades, you will need to act quickly. Clearing starts straight away, so don't waste any time – get hold of a list of unfilled places and contact the universities direct. You will be sent instructions on Clearing automatically. UCAS has now introduced a new scheme called Adjustment which allows students who have performed significantly better than they had expected a short period to approach universities that require higher grades than the offer they were holding. See 'Results day' below for further details.

■ The Personal Statement

The Personal Statement section of the UCAS application is the only chance you get to convince the selectors that they should allocate one of their precious places to you, or call you for an interview. It is therefore important to take great care in writing the Personal Statement so that you can convince them that:

- you are serious about studying psychology
- you have researched the course and the career options
- you will be able to contribute to the department and the university.

Obviously, there are as many ways of writing a Personal Statement as there are candidates. There are no rules as such, but there are recommendations that can be made. Universities are academic institutions and thus you must present yourself as a strong academic bet. The admissions tutor reading your form will want to know all the relevant information about you and will want some answers to the following questions:

- **What started your interest in psychology?** This might have been because of a book or article you read, a TV programme, or through contact with a family friend who worked in the field. It might have been because you chose psychology as one of your AS levels. Again, there is no 'right' reason, but the selectors will be interested in what started you on the path to your application.

- **What have you done to investigate psychology?** This is your chance to show that this application is not just a whim on your part, but the result of serious research. Many students think that psychology is only about interpretation of dreams or why someone is attracted to someone else, rather than a serious and rigorous academic subject. You have to differentiate yourself from them by showing the selectors that you have thought carefully about what a psychology course and/or career involves. You could mention books that you have read, lectures you have been to, or relevant work experience or work shadowing. You could also write about the subjects you are studying at school and how they will useful when you are at university.
- **How can you contribute to the department and the university?** To show that you are going to fit in well at the institution, and add to the life of the university, you can write about your non-academic achievements, extra-curricular activities, and anything else that will show that you have something to offer.

Work experience is very useful, as it demonstrates a commitment to the subject outside the classroom, so remember to mention any experience, paid or voluntary. Explain what your job entailed and what you got out of the whole experience. Even if you haven't been able to get work experience, if you have spoken to anyone in the psychology profession about their job, then it is worth mentioning, as it all builds up a picture of someone who is keen and has done some research. If you have had relevant work experience, write about it on your form. Explain concisely what your job entailed, for example:

> During the summer vacation, I volunteered at a summer camp for children with learning disabilities. This has been a most valuable experience and I thoroughly enjoyed working with the children, particularly because I was able to appreciate much better some of the work that we have covered in developmental and cognitive psychology in my A level course.

Future plans can also be included, if you have them. Again, be precise and informative. This will demonstrate a breadth of interest in the subject.

The first thing that the admissions tutor wants to know is the strength of your commitment to study. Say clearly why you wish to study for your chosen degree, especially if you haven't studied psychology before. Wanting to work with people, or liking children, is not good enough. Give details of particular areas of study that interest you and say what you hope to get out of researching them at university level. Bookshops have sections on 'popular psychology' which contain books about psychology for non-psychologists – this is a good starting point if you wish to demonstrate an interest in the subject but haven't studied it at AS or A level. A word of warning: don't try to impress the selectors by claiming that you have read degree-level psychology books, as you may get asked about your reading if you are called for interview – stick to things that you can understand and discuss. A selection of titles is listed at the end of this book in the section on psychology texts to get you started. If you have particularly enjoyed certain parts of your AS or A level Psychology course, say so – and explain why. If you are new to the subject, give examples from newspapers, television events or controversies that have appealed to the psychologist in you.

At least 60% of your Personal Statement should deal with material directly related to your chosen course. Thereafter, use the rest of the page to tell the admissions tutor what makes you who you are. What travel have you undertaken? What music do you like and/or play? What do you read? What sporting achievements do you have? In all these things give details.

The example below is weak.

> Last year I went to France. I like reading and listening to music and sometimes I play football at weekends.

A stronger version might read:

> Last year I drove through France and enjoyed visiting the chateaux of the Loire. I relax by reading the novels of Stephen King and have hardback first editions of all his books. My musical taste is extremely wide, ranging from Gregorian Chant to Robbie Williams, and I would like to continue playing the cello in an orchestra at university. I would also be keen to play in a football team to keep myself fit.

Don't expect to be able to fit everything about yourself in the limited space available, and only include things that you are prepared to expand on at interview. The idea is to whet their appetite and to make them want to meet you.

What do I look for in a UCAS Personal Statement? First and foremost, evidence of research into psychology. I will not automatically reject someone who only mentions Freud and/or relationships but this needs to be backed up with some serious reading or work experience. I do not expect students to be reading university textbooks but they should make a habit of looking at new developments in psychology on relevant websites, and reading books

*about, for example, how the brain works. Students who study
psychology at A level can write about their research projects to
show that they been thinking independently.*

Admissions Tutor

A sample Personal Statement

I first became aware of the work of a psychologist when my nephew
was diagnosed with attention deficiency hyperactive disorder, and I
was able to see how his life was changed because of the treatment
and help that he received. I hope that, by studying psychology, I will
be able to provide treatment and support for children with developmental disorders so that they too can have a bright future and opportunities equivalent to those of any other children.

As I am not taking psychology at A level, I have tried to make sure
that I have sufficient background knowledge as preparation for my
degree course. I have read books such as 'A First Course In Psychology' and 'The Brain' by Susan Greenfield. These books have
deepened my interest in pursuing psychology, in particular clinical
psychology. For A level, I am taking Biology, Chemistry and Mathematics. Therefore, I am familiar with the need for scientific and objec-
tive experimental procedures involved in psychological research and
experiments. Biology at A level has given me a good understanding
on the anatomy of humans and animals and its relevance to the
nature versus nurture debate that has been ongoing between nativist
psychologists and empiricist psychologists. Since psychology
involves the study of behaviour and experience, chemistry at A level
will help me comprehend the relation between hormonal changes
and the human behaviour. Statistics is a fundamental tool for psychologists in assessing the validity of experimental results, and I
particularly enjoy this aspect of A level Mathematics.

To gain insight into the world of medicine and science, I organised
attachments at a hospital and a biotechnology farm. Working with a
surgeon, I observed the dedication and hard work that is required
from the hospital staff to be successful in a medical career. Most
importantly, they had a tremendous amount of patience that is clearly
needed when dealing with patients. I believe the same principles
apply for a career in psychology, in particular when dealing with children. During that period, I had the chance to meet doctors and nurses
and listen to what their average day in a hospital is like, as well as
general information on how they deal with patients to make them as
comfortable as possible. I was particularly aware of the need to balance analytical skills and scientific knowledge with an understanding
of the patients' emotional needs. My second attachment was with a

pioneering biotechnology farm, involved in the production of high-quality livestock genetics material. Its production of animal genetics material allowed me to observe embryo transfer and artificial insemination being performed on Boer Goats.

For my Duke of Edinburgh's Gold Award I took part in an expedition which taught me invaluable social skills such as leadership and teamwork. In addition to these activities, I carried out various fund-raising projects for orphanages, hospitals' paediatric wards and victims of natural disasters. The most successful one was a fund-raising and awareness campaign for lupus, a chronic autoimmune disease mainly affecting women of non-European descent. From this, I learned what real working life is like, as I had to deal with corporate and individual sponsors as well as non-government organisations.

For leisure, I enjoy swimming, horse riding and golf. I learnt ballet and performed at shows, before a serious ankle injury forced me to give up. My involvement in horse riding and ballet taught me not just discipline and hard work; I also learnt that perseverance is the key to achieving my dreams. I also play the piano and have completed it to Grade 7.

General tips

- Do not attempt to copy passages from other sources. UCAS checks Personal Statements with anti-plagiarism software: if you have used material from someone else you will be caught out and your application will be cancelled.
- Don't be tempted to get someone else to write your Personal Statement. It has to sound like **you**, which is why it is called a *Personal Statement*.
- Although you can apply for up to five institutions or courses, you only write one Personal Statement, and so it needs to be relevant to all of the courses you are applying for. You will not be able to write a convincing statement if you are applying to a variety of different courses (see below).
- Print off a copy of your Personal Statement so that you can remind yourself of all the wonderful things you said, should you be called for interview!
- If you are planning to do so, state your reasons for applying for deferred entry and outline what you intend to do during your gap year. For example, you might be planning to find some relevant work experience in a hospital, and then spend some time overseas to brush up your language skills.

> ### Warning: mixing courses and Joint Honours courses
>
> You write **one** Personal Statement which is read by admissions staff at the **five** courses for which you are applying. Each university only sees its name and course code on the form that UCAS sends to it: your other choices are not shown. If, for example, you are applying to read psychology at one university, neuroscience at another, history at a third, and so on, then you cannot possibly write a Personal Statement that will satisfy the criteria for each of the courses. The psychology selector will wonder why you have written about history, and so on. The likelihood is that you will be rejected by all of your choices.
>
> Similarly, if you apply for a Joint Honours course such as psychology and sociology, your form will be seen by selectors from both departments, each of whom will want to see that you are a serious candidate for his/her course.
>
> Many universities offer very detailed advice about what they are looking for in a Personal Statement, and some will reject you if your statement does not conform to what they are looking for. Even if you are not going to apply there, the London School of Economics website contains some very useful advice on writing Personal Statements (www.lse.ac.uk).

Non-standard applications

Mature students

Mature students (in general, applicants who are over the age of 21) generally fall into three categories.

1| Those with A level (or equivalent) grades that are sufficient for entry onto a psychology degree course, but who have been working or have been involved in other activities since they completed their studies. For these students, all of the advice in the previous chapters is applicable. They would need to apply through UCAS, as previously described. The main difference might be in the 'Employment' section of the form, where more detail will be required, and in the Personal Statement, which should contain an overview of what the candidate has been doing since he or she sat their school exams.

2| Those who have already studied at university, but in a different subject. For these students, there are a number of choices which will depend on why they are looking at the option of a psychology degree. If the eventual aim is to qualify as a chartered psychologist, they should take advice from the BPS about their possible options. In some cases, it may be necessary to study psychology at degree level, but it might be possible to undertake further postgraduate training without the need to do this.

3| Those without the necessary qualifications to be accepted onto a degree course. Potential applicants in this position should contact university admissions departments to discuss their individual situations. They may be advised to take A levels (or equivalent), possibly on an accelerated one-year course offered by some sixth-form colleges, or there may be Access or Foundation courses that are more appropriate.

The importance of the Personal Statement and CV for mature student applications

Although a certain amount of factual information will be available to the selectors through reading the UCAS form (education details, qualifications, employment details etc.), it is important that they are able to understand fully the route that the mature applicant has taken to get to the point that he or she is applying for psychology courses. As one admissions tutor says: *'What I want to see is a narrative of the events and decisions that led to the application. Why apply now? What have you been doing since you were at school? What caused the change in direction?'*

Some of this can be explained in the Personal Statement. For example:

> After I sat my A levels in 2002, I started an English Literature degree course at Bristol University. However, I soon realised that this was not the right option for me, so I withdrew and started work in a local accountant's office as an administrator. At that time I also did some voluntary work at a local care home, and it was this that began my interest in medical issues, and in particular, psychology. To research the subject further, I . . .

If you cannot tell the whole story using the UCAS form and Personal Statement, then put together a CV and send it directly to the admissions departments. They will then attach this to your UCAS form. In order to ensure that they can match up the CV with your application, send the CV **after** you have been given your application number from UCAS, and quote this in all correspondence with the universities.

The CV should include details of all employment, and should fill in any gaps.

> **June 2003–April 2006: Fletcher and Anderson Accountants, Pymore, Dorset**
>
> Office Administrator (Full-time) – duties included managing client appointments, filing documents, maintaining stationery supplies.

August 2003–April 2006: West Bay Care Home, Dorset

Volunteer (two evenings a week and Sundays) – helping to wash and feed patients. Talking to them and contacting relatives on their behalf.

April 2006–January 2007: travelling in South and South East Asia

During this period, I volunteered at a primary school in north Thailand for three weeks. My main task was to help the children to learn English.

International students

Students who are from outside the UK need to apply for psychology courses in the same way as UK students – using the online UCAS form (www.ucas.com). The UCAS website contains a section for international students which describes the process and the deadlines in detail. The 'Education' section of the UCAS form contains drop-down menus of many international qualifications, not just UK exams.

International students can often be at a disadvantage, not because they are applying from overseas but because they or their advisers are not as familiar with what the selectors at UK universities are looking for in a strong application. This affects two sections of the application:

1| the Personal Statement
2| the Reference.

The Personal Statement for international students

The UCAS Personal Statement needs to focus on the course itself, and what the student has done to investigate it. The advice given in Chapter 4 is equally applicable to international students, and should be read carefully. It is important to remember that the student is 'selling' him- or herself to the admissions staff by demonstrating suitability for the course, not on personal achievements or qualities.

References

Often, a promising application is rejected because the person providing the reference is unfamiliar with what is required, and the selectors have no choice other than to reject because they are not given enough information. UCAS references need to focus on the following:

- the student's suitability for the course and level of study
- an assessment of the student's academic performance to date (including the student's level of English if this is not his or her first language).
- how the student will adapt to studying in the UK
- the student's personal qualities.

If you are unsure as to whether the person who will write your reference fully understands what is required, show them the section on the UCAS website called 'Non-UK Advisers'.

05 Succeeding in your interview

You may not get called for interview at all, since only a few of the universities now conduct formal interviews. However, a number of universities – usually those with the highest ratio of applicants per place – still ask students to attend a formal interview, and others combine Open Days with more informal meetings. If you do apply to a university that interviews applicants, don't worry: the interview is a chance for you to demonstrate to the selectors your suitability for the course. It will not be an unpleasant experience as long as you do your preparation.

■ General hints for interviews

While the number of people conducting the interview and the length of time it takes can vary, all interviews are designed to enable those asking the questions to find out as much about the candidate as they can. It is important, therefore, to engage actively with the process (good eye contact and confident body language help) and treat it as a chance to put yourself across rather than as an obstacle course trying to catch you out.

Interviewers are more interested in what you know than in what you don't know. If you are asked something you can't answer, say so. To waffle (or worse, to lie) simply wastes time and lets you down. The interviewers will be considering the quality of thought that goes into your answers; they will not expect you to know everything already.

> Pauses while you think are perfectly acceptable; don't be afraid to take your time.

It is likely that one, or more, of the interviewers will be your tutor(s) during your time at university. Enthusiasm for, a strong commitment to, and a willingness to learn your chosen subject are all extremely important attitudes to convey. The people you meet at interview not only have to judge your academic calibre, but also have to decide whether they would enjoy teaching you for the next three to four years. Try to demonstrate your enthusiasm by mentioning books or articles that you have read, or topics that you enjoyed as part of your AS or A level Psychology course.

An ability to think on your feet is vital. Pre-learned responses never work: they appear glib and superficial and, no matter how apparently spontaneously they are delivered, they are always detectable. Putting forward an answer step by step, using examples and factual knowledge to reinforce your points, is far more professional, even if you are not completely sure of what you are saying. That said, it is also sensible to admit defeat: knowing you are beaten is a more intelligent thing than mindlessly clinging to the wreckage of a specious case.

It is possible to steer the interview yourself to some extent. If, for example, you are asked to comment on something you know little about, confidently replacing the question with another related one shows enthusiasm. Don't waste time in silences that are as embarrassing for the panel as for the candidate.

Essential preparation includes revision of the Personal Statement from your UCAS application. This may well form the basis of preliminary questions (which are meant to put you at your ease) and if it proves to be a mass of fabrications, the interview is doomed from the start!

Questions may well be asked about your extra-curricular activities. Again, this is to put you at your ease: your answers should be thorough and enthusiastic, but not too long! Some more specific psychology-related questions are listed below.

At the end of the interview you are normally given a chance to ask questions of your own. If you have none, say that the interview has covered all the queries you had. It is sensible, though, to have one or two questions of a serious kind – about the course, the tuition, etc. – up your sleeve. Don't ask anything that you could, and should, have found answers to in the prospectus. It is also fine, even desirable, to base a question on the interview itself. This marks you out as someone who listens, is curious and who is keen to learn.

Above all, make them remember you when they go through a list of 20 or more applicants at the end of the day.

■ Specimen interview questions

1| Why have you chosen to study psychology?
2| What first interested you in psychology?
3| What do you understand by the word 'psychology'?
4| What do psychologists do?
5| What would you like to do after graduating?
6| What are the differences between psychology, psychiatry and psychotherapy?
7| What have you done to investigate psychology?
8| Why did you/didn't you choose to study psychology at AS or A level?

9| Have you read any books on psychology?

10| What particular areas of psychology interest you?

11| How do you keep up with current issues in psychology?

12| Tell me about something that is related to psychology that has been in the newspapers recently.

13| New theories in psychology need to be tested: how do psychologists go about testing theories?

14| Give me an example of an experiment which tests a psychological theory.

15| Is it ethical to experiment on human subjects?

16| Describe some of the links between biology and psychology.

17| Why is a knowledge of mathematics important when studying psychology?

18| Who should judge whether someone has a psychological disorder?

19| How do you cope with stress?

20| How do you relax?

21| What are your best/worst qualities?

22| I see from your Personal Statement that you are interested in (insert topic/interest). Tell me about it.

23| What are you going to do in your gap year?

24| Why are you taking a gap year?

25| Why did you apply here?

26| What do you like about our psychology course?

27| What options will you choose in the second year?

28| Why did you choose a Joint Honours degree?

When we interview students we want to reassure ourselves that we are not going waste a place on him or her. So, in order to convince us, the interviewee needs to have looked at our course in detail and be prepared to tell us what aspects of it are attractive; he or she should have good reasons for choosing the university (coming to an Open Day is always a plus point); and he or she should have looked beyond the degree at career routes for psychology graduates.

Admissions Tutor

Finding the facts

Although admissions interviews are not offered routinely by all universities, staff will try to ensure that applicants have a chance to visit the course centre to find out more about the learning environment. Some, for example, will offer group interviews in which a member of staff will lead a discussion about the degree programme, enabling applicants to ask questions about the course. Others will host Open Days and campus tours which provide applicants with the chance of talking to current students about the 'student experience' and viewing the university's facilities.

You should take every opportunity to visit the higher education institutions to which you are applying because, in themselves, prospectus entries will only give you part of the picture. The checklist below will give you an idea of the kinds of questions to ask when you visit a university or college to find out more about a particular course.

■ Questions you need to ask

About entry

1| What additional information is available about the course of study, apart from that in the prospectus?
2| What are the aims and objectives of the course?
3| What size is the first year intake?
4| What entry grades are required? How strictly are these kept to?

About study and learning

5| Apart from courses in psychology, what other ancillary courses will I need to take?
6| What are the class-contact hours for first year students?
7| How much time will I have for private study?
8| What are the main teaching activities?
9| Over the duration of the programme, what proportion of my time will I spend in lectures, seminars, practicals, project work and placements?
10| Will it help if I have my own personal computer?

About assessment and learning support

11| Will I have a personal tutor?
12| Are there specific courses in study methods?
13| How will my work be assessed?
14| Will my first-year results count towards the final degree result?
15| Are there opportunities to have coaching/mentoring from more experienced students?
16| What happens if students fail their first year?

About career opportunities and employment

17| Do present students receive help in finding part-time work to help pay for the cost of accommodation, fees, etc.?
18| Is the course recognised by the BPS, giving the GBC?
19| Where does the degree course lead in terms of career opportunities and further study?
20| What links do lecturers have with employers and practising professional psychologists?

21| Are there particular course modules designed to help students with their career decisions?

These questions are largely concerned with the student experience from the perspective of academic study. Prospective students are, in addition, likely to have a range of other questions concerning accommodation, finance and the kind of facilities each university has to offer.

The interview itself: general tips

- Make sure you arrive early.
- Dress comfortably, but show that you are taking the interview seriously: wear smart, clean clothes.
- Make eye contact.
- Be willing to listen as well as talk, and don't be afraid to ask questions if you are unsure of what the interviewer wants.
- Be willing to consider new ideas, if your interview involves discussion of psychology issues.
- Be yourself.
- Above all, be enthusiastic.

HOPE

Use the acronym HOPE to remind yourself of the personal qualities that you should try to display at the interview:

H Honesty

O Open-mindedness

P Preparedness

E Enthusiasm.

Getting your place and finding funding

■ Results day

Achieving the grades for your Firm choice

If you are holding a Conditional offer from your Firm choice, and you have got the grades that you need, then you do not need to do anything. Your chosen university will already have the results, and will in due course send you information about when the course starts, accommodation and other practicalities. To check that you have been accepted, you can log on to the Track facility on the UCAS website.

If you have done significantly better than you had anticipated, and wish to look at university courses that required higher grades than your original offer, you can register for Adjustment, which is a system that allows you to hold on to your original offer for a short period whilst at the same time investigating other courses. Details can be found on the UCAS website.

A summary of the options available when you receive your results is shown below.

You have . . .	What can happen	What you need to do
. . . gained grades that are close to those required for your Firm choice (e.g. BBB for an ABB offer), and satisfy your Insurance offer.	Your Firm choice can still accept you. Otherwise, you are automatically accepted onto the Insurance place.	Check on Track to see if you have been accepted. If not, contact the university and see if they can be persuaded to accept you. Your referee might be able to help with this.
. . . grades that are not close to those required for your Firm choice, but satisfy your Insurance offer.	You are automatically accepted onto the Insurance place.	Check on Track to see if the Insurance offer has been confirmed.
. . . grades that are below those needed for the Insurance offer.	You are now eligible for Clearing.	Use the UCAS website and national newspapers to identify suitable courses from the published vacancies. Contact them by telephone.

(Continued)

You have . . .	What can happen	What you need to do
. . . grades that satisfy one of your offers, but you have changed your mind about the course you want to study.	You can be considered for Clearing courses if you withdraw from your Firm/Insurance places.	Contact UCAS to withdraw from your original place. Use the UCAS website and national newspapers to identify suitable courses from the published vacancies. Contact them by telephone.
. . . achieved grades that are not good enough to get you a Clearing place.	You can be accepted onto Access or Foundation places, and then progress on to a degree course. Alternatively, you can resit A levels and reapply next year.	Discuss these options with parents and/or careers advisors.
. . . done better than expected, and you have grades that match or exceed the standard offers for courses that you had not previously applied for; perhaps because you did not think that you would be considered by these universities because of your grade predictions.	You have a short period of time to register for Adjustment. This means that you hold on to your original offer but can also approach other universities to see if they have suitable vacancies that you could be considered for.	Log onto Track to register. Start telephoning universities.

Full details can be found on the UCAS website.

■ Extenuating circumstances

If issues such as illness, family problems or other problems during the examination sitting affected your grades, make sure that you have written confirmation of this (such as a letter from a doctor, solicitor or someone at your school or college) and fax or scan and email this to the admissions department for your chosen course. Ideally, if something does go wrong at the time you are sitting your exams, you or the school/college should inform the universities immediately, warning them that you might not achieve the grades. It is more likely that they can make concessions then rather than when they have already made decisions about who to accept when the results are issued.

■ When you have your place . . .

Once you have secured a place at university you will need to think about fees and funding. Below is a breakdown of the different fee systems across the UK as well as the funding available.

Undergraduate courses: fees and funding

All UK and EU students pay tuition fees of up to £3,225 per year (2009 entry) as a contribution towards the cost of the course. Some students will have up to 100% of this paid by their local authority, depending on the income of their parents. Details of how these grants are calculated can be found on the Directgov website (address at the end of this book).

Even if you are not eligible for a grant, your fees do not have to be paid whilst you are studying – you can take out a loan which does not have to start being repaid until you are working and earning more than £15,000 per year.

Scottish students who choose a Scottish university or art college do not pay any tuition fees.

Welsh students studying in Wales will be charged up to £3,225 a year, but will receive a grant (non-repayable) of up to £1,940 per year to off-set the fees. The UCAS website has full details of fees and support arrangements (www.ucas.com).

Students from Northern Ireland who are applying to institutions within Northern Ireland should consult www.studentfinanceni.co.uk for details of what fees they will be expected to pay, and the help that they might receive.

Students on higher education courses are eligible to apply for student loans to help with living costs. Students can borrow up to about £10,000 per year.

Many universities have scholarships and bursaries available. These can take many forms and are administered by the universities themselves. Some are subject specific, whilst others are more general. They can be awarded for academic excellence, for cases of financial hardship, and for students from particular countries. For example, UCL offers a range of scholarships and bursaries including:

- the UCL Global Excellence Scholarship (£5,000) for prospective undergraduates
- the Professor Denys Holland and Cowan Cheung Scholarship (£10,000) for students from Hong Kong and other regions of China
- the Denys Holland Undergraduate Scholarship (£9,300) for students facing financial hardship.

For detailed information about all scholarships and bursaries available at universities across the UK read *University Scholarships, Awards & Bursaries* by Brian Heap (Trotman).

Funding for postgraduate courses

There is no automatic right to funding or student loans for this type of course. Students are often self-funding – or may be assisted by scholarships from universities or from other organisations. Contacting the institution to which you are applying is a good way to begin exploring your options.

Other sources of funding

Commercial organisations, charitable trusts, educational institutions and government agencies all offer sponsorship, special grants, access funds and scholarships, but these sources of finance are limited and hard to come by. If you are facing financial difficulties, a good place to start looking for information is the college that you are applying to.

The UCAS website contains a section on funding, with contact details and links to a number of funding bodies.

Funding for international students

EU students pay the same tuition fees as UK students (see above). These fees are subsidised by the UK government or the EU. Students from outside of the EU pay the full university tuition fees, which can range from £10,000 per year up to £18,000 per year. Accommodation and food will be extra. Some UK universities have scholarships available for international students. You should go to the 'international' sections on the university websites for more details. Many governments and charities offer scholarships for students to allow them to study in the UK. You should contact your local education department to see if they have contact details.

07 Psychology courses across the UK

U se this section to read a bit more about each of the places on your shortlist. They are arranged alphabetically and each one gives a contact address. The information has been provided by the universities. Information on BPS accreditation is given in each university's entry, and also in the table on pages 97–8. You should always check the university websites and prospectuses before making an application, as the courses available, course content and entrance requirements may change.

ABERDEEN

The University of Aberdeen
Regent Walk
Aberdeen AB24 3FX
Tel: 01224 272000
http://aberdeen.ac.uk/psychology/

Aberdeen offers Psychology as a Single Honours degree under both BSc and MA degree schemes. It can also be studied as Combined Honours with a modern language, and as a Joint Honours with computing science, anthropology, philosophy, sociology or statistics. The Scottish degree structure provides breadth and flexibility in the early stages, so that the final choice of degree does not have to be made until the end of the second year. Progress to junior Honours (level 3) is dependent on good performance in the levels 1 and 2 psychology assessments.

The level 3 curriculum includes courses on methodology, biopsychology, perception, developmental psychology, human memory and social psychology. In level 4 students have a choice of options, and carry out and report on an empirical investigation. Students can apply to study abroad for part of their degree under European or North American exchange programmes. The Honours degrees are accredited by the BPS.

ABERTAY DUNDEE

University of Abertay Dundee
Bell Street
Dundee DD1 1HG
Tel: 01382 308000
www.abertay.ac.uk/Schools/SHS/psychology_info.cfm

The University of Abertay Dundee has two degree programmes that are accredited by the BPS as conferring eligibility for graduate membership with GBCC. From the 2006 intake, accreditation is subject to the requirement that the minimum standard of qualification of a second class Honours is achieved. The accredited BSc (Hons) Psychology course offers two foundation years covering psychology, research methods and sociology. Students specialise in psychology in the final two years. In addition to all the core areas of the BPS curriculum, the programme offers a range of psychology options in the third and fourth years, which may include:

- animal psychology
- applied psychology
- clinical psychology (with contributions from clinical practitioners)
- community psychology
- forensic psychology
- health psychology
- neuropsychology
- psychology in education
- psychopharmacology
- specialist topics in cognitive and developmental psychology
- sport psychology.

All final-year students submit a supervised psychology project in an area of their own interest.

The accredited BSc (Hons) Forensic Psychobiology course covers core areas of psychology with other disciplines. Compared with the BSc Psychology, Forensic Psychobiology has greater focus on psychological explanations of criminal behaviour and allows students to explore specialist subjects in forensic science and biology. Psychology also forms a large part of the BSc (Hons) in Behavioural Science and, to a lesser extent, of the BA (Hons) in Social Science. However, these two programmes are not BPS accredited. Note that students on the BSc Psychology, BSc Behavioural Science and BSc Sociology courses can transfer freely among these three programmes during the first two years. The Psychology Department is actively involved in research and has excellent research laboratories, which students can use for their final-year projects. There are specialist research laboratories offering, for example, behaviour observation, eye-tracking, vision research facilities, human factors research facilities and speech analysis, along with a range of other experimental psychology research facilities. The university has excellent library and computing facilities, and the Psychology Department has its own recently upgraded teaching laboratories.

ANGLIA RUSKIN

Anglia Ruskin University
East Road

Cambridge CB1 1PT
Tel: 0845 271333
www.anglia.co.uk

Despite its relatively short history, the Department of Psychology at Anglia Ruskin has been very successful so far. The teaching provision was rated as 'Excellent' at the latest Teaching Quality Assessment (TQA) by the Quality Assurance Agency (QAA), and the Single Honours psychology course is fully accredited by the BPS. The main topics will include social, cognitive, developmental and health psychology as well as relevant research methods.

Students are asked to evaluate theories and research methodologies critically and to keep abreast of relevant philosophical debates, issues and controversies. You will have the opportunity to carry out investigations using a variety of methods, including experimental work, interviews and observational studies. Opportunities are provided for group work in discussions, project work and presentations. The final-year project will enable you to develop your skills by conducting an independent piece of research.

ASTON

Aston University
Aston Triangle
Birmingham B4 7ET
Tel: 0121 359 3611
www.aston.ac.uk/lhs

You can choose between three-year and four-year sandwich BSc Human Psychology degree programmes, both conferring eligibility for graduate membership of the BPS. The four-year sandwich programme includes a 12-month professional work placement between year two and the final year. Over half of Aston's psychology students take a placement year and it is especially recommended for those seeking a professional career in psychology, in clinical psychology for example.

Students can switch between the three- and four-year programmes so a final decision about whether or not to take a placement need not be taken at application. Psychology can be taken as 50% of a Combined Honours degree in combination with a wide range of subjects. Combinations with biology, sociology, a language and business are popular but combined degrees do not confer eligibility for graduate membership of the BPS. There is a wide range of final-year options enabling students to tailor their studies to fit their own interests and career path. Aston emphasises the human and the applied aspects of psychology and graduate employability. Aston psychology teaching is officially rated as 'Excellent' and the department has a strong record (grade 5), especially in neuroscience. As the human psychology degree gives you a grounding in the human and social sciences, familiarity with carrying out and evaluating research and the statistical treatment of data, a high degree of literacy and an ability to argue a case (psychology is never a cut and dried subject), graduates are able to enter a very wide range of careers in addition to professional psychology.

BANGOR

Bangor University
Bangor LL57 2DG
Tel: 01248 382629
www.bangor.ac.uk/psychology

As the third-largest Psychology School in the UK Bangor employs modern teaching methods in a friendly environment that students value. Bangor won a recent *Times* student support poll, and topped the 'most helpful' category in the 2007 first-year student survey. Bangor's teaching has been awarded the highest possible grade of 'Excellent' by the Government's QAA. Bangor Psychology was rated 7th in the UK in the 2008 RAE. The courses available are:

- BSc/BA (Hons) Psychology
- BSc (Hons) Psychology with Clinical and Health Psychology
- BSc (Hons) Psychology with Child and Language Development
- BSc (Hons) Psychology with Neuropsychology.

In 2007 two-thirds of graduates from the BPS fully accredited degree programmes obtained a First Class or a 2:1 Honours degree.

BATH

The University of Bath
Claverton Down
Bath BA2 7AY
Tel: 01225 388388
www.bath.ac.uk/psychology

Bath provides a four-year sandwich course in psychology, which is accredited by the BPS as conferring eligibility for graduate membership with GBC. The course gives a grounding across the discipline, with a particular focus on social, health, developmental and cognitive psychology. Students will also be expected to take courses from the following options: sociology and social policy, a modern language or biology. Final-year options can be all psychology or a combination from the above options. These are taught by staff who are actively researching in these areas. Examples currently include economic and political psychology, health and artificial intelligence, and controversies in cognition. Assessment is approximately 50% coursework and 50% examination.

The department emphasises the importance of training students in marketable and transferable skills, and students are required to spend their third year on placements (probably unpaid) in one of a wide range of settings within professional psychology (for example clinical, educational, occupational or research) either in the UK or overseas. Most final-year dissertations arise out of research work done during the placement. Students find the placement year invaluable as a preparation for career choice.

BATH SPA

Bath Spa University College
Newton Park
Bath BA2 9BN
Tel: 01225 875875
www.bathspa.ac.uk/schools/social-sciences

Bath Spa offers psychology as Single, Joint, major or minor BSc/BA under the combined scheme. In addition to traditional areas of study, it offers a wide range of optional modules, including neuropsychology, criminological psychology and evolutionary psychology, allowing psychology specialists to develop their interests. The Single Honours course is accredited by the BPS.

BEDFORDSHIRE

University of Bedfordshire
Park Square
Luton LU1 3JV
Tel: 01582 489 286
www.beds.ac.uk

Psychology has gained accreditation by the BPS for all undergraduate courses (accreditation for the BSc Psychology and Criminal Behaviour is being sought) and for the MSc Health Psychology. Furthermore, the QAA rated the teaching quality of all courses 'Excellent'. The department has an international staff body with extensive research and teaching interests in all aspects of psychology, but with a particular emphasis on important and exciting areas such as health and mental health psychology and the psychology of learning.

BIRMINGHAM

The University of Birmingham
Birmingham B15 2TT
Tel: 0121 414 4933
www.bham.ac.uk/psychology

Birmingham's School of Psychology is a strong department which is ranked third in the UK behind Oxford and Cambridge for internationally excellent research, following the recent RAE. The school is internationally recognised for its teaching and research and has close relationships with local hospitals, clinics, schools, industrial companies and departments of local and national government. The BSc (Hons) degree programme consists of a range of compulsory modules for the first two years, which cover core areas of contemporary psychology. In the final year, students are able to choose four modules to enable specialisation in areas of interest, e.g. forensic psychology or intellectual disability. The school will be introducing a fourth year to its BSc (Hons) degree, with effect from 2010, which leads to a MSc in Psychology. More details of this course can be found on the school's website. Both courses are accredited by the BPS as conferring eligibility for graduate membership with GBC.

BOLTON

The University of Bolton
Dean Road
Bolton BL3 5AB
Tel: 01204 903903
www.bolton.ac.uk/pls

The University of Bolton offers Single Honours courses in criminological and forensic psychology, counselling and psychology, and sport and exercise psychology. It also offers a BSc (Hons) Psychology course that may be studied in single, major or joint modes. All these courses are accredited by the BPS as conferring eligibility for graduate membership with GBC. The modular degree scheme offers students both mandatory and optional modules. Students study six modules each year (three per semester), which cover all aspects of psychology. In the final year each student conducts an individual research project as well as studying specialised modules. Teaching and research accommodation includes lecture theatres, laboratories, computer suites and a video laboratory.

BOURNEMOUTH

Bournemouth University
Studland House
12 Christchurch Road
Bournemouth BH1 3NA
Tel: 01202 524111
www.dec.bournemouth.ac.uk

It is important today that those who are interested in human behaviour know something about technological systems – how they can be used to help people, and how their design can be improved to this end. Conversely, people of a more technological inclination need to know something about the people who will use or otherwise be affected by their designs. The three-year BSc Applied Psychology and Computing course examines the interaction of psychological and computing factors in the development of effective, safe and satisfying computer systems. The university is currently seeking BPS accreditation for this programme.

BRADFORD

University of Bradford
Bradford BD7 1DP
Tel: 01274 233515
www.bradford.ac.uk/acad/psychology

The University of Bradford offers a number of psychology degrees. The BSc (Hons)/BA Psychology programme is accredited by the BPS as conferring eligibility for graduate membership with GBC. As a student of psychology at Bradford you will develop many skills that will allow you to understand the brain, society and the individuals that exist around you on a daily basis. These skills will be developed in the Centre of Psychology Studies' new purpose-built laboratories which include: language and cognitive psychology laboratory; an experimental cubicle suite, equipped with PC and experiment-generation software; interview suite; and an observation suite with two-way mirror and digital image/audio equipment. The course structure ensures a broad coverage of psychology and some of the exciting options that you may wish to study include:

- advanced issues in neuropsychology
- evolutionary psychology
- forensic psychology
- psychological disorders and treatment interventions.

Bradford also offers BA courses in: psychology and crime; psychology and management; sociology and psychology and interdisciplinary human studies. These courses are not currently accredited by the BPS.

BRISTOL

University of Bristol
Senate House
Bristol BS8 1TH
Tel: 0117 928 9000
http://psychology.psy.bris.ac.uk

The Bristol Psychology Department has active links with other departments including child health and sport, exercise and health sciences and with the Burden Neurological Institute. Bristol offers a BSc in Experimental Psychology in the Sciences and Joint Honours degrees in psychology with zoology. Both the Single and the Joint Honours programmes are accredited by the BPS. In the final year, students are encouraged to present reports of projects at an annual South West Area Student Conference.

BRISTOL UWE

University of the West of England
Faculty of Applied Sciences (Psychology)
Frenchay Campus
Coldharbour Lane
Bristol BS16 1QY
Tel: 0117 328 3333 (Enquiry and Admissions Service)
www.science.uwe.ac.uk/psychology

The BSc (Hons) Psychology at UWE is fully accredited by the BPS, covering most of the required aspects of the curriculum during years 1 and 2. A particular strength of the course is the wide variety of optional modules available at level 3. These currently include:

- advanced developmental psychology
- cognitive neuropsychology
- counselling theory and practice
- critical psychology
- critical sexualities
- developmental psychopathology
- gender and psychology
- health psychology
- identities in social psychology
- individual differences in development
- issues in the psychology of education
- issues in the psychology of work
- language and mind
- learning disabilities
- perception
- psychological issues in mental health

- psychology and evolution
- psychology of addiction
- psychology of consciousness
- psychology of religion
- psychology of sport and exercise
- psychometrics and psychological test construction
- psychopharmacology
- qualitative research methods.

Additionally, students can opt to follow named awards in:

- applied psychology
- biological psychology
- health psychology
- psychology and mental health
- social psychology.

This involves selecting module options which relate to one of the above-mentioned areas and carrying out a research project in that field. Details of other, non-BPS accredited study options which include psychology can be found on the UWE website.

BRUNEL

Brunel University
Uxbridge UB8 3PH
Tel: 01895 274000
www.brunel.ac.uk/about/acad/sssl

Students can study either for a BSc in Psychology or for a BSc Joint Honours combining Psychology with Sociology or Social Anthropology. Both Single and Joint Honours psychology degrees are BPS accredited. The early stage of the course involves a multidisciplinary approach, which is followed by opportunities to specialise. Teaching is heavily influenced by research interests of staff. Both three-year full-time and four-year thin-sandwich modes of study are available. The thin-sandwich degree is designed to link academic theory with work experience gained over two separate placements. The department helps students find suitable placements, some of which are paid. However, students are also encouraged to pursue their own placements, particularly if they would like to go abroad.

BUCKINGHAM

University of Buckingham
Hunter Street
Buckingham MK18 1EG
Tel: 01280 814080
www.buckingham.ac.uk/psychology

The Psychology Department at the University of Buckingham offers two-year BSc degrees in psychology with two entry points – January and September (two and a quarter years). The structure of degree programmes at Buckingham means that they cover the same number of weeks in two years as other universities do in three. Students are able to study psychology alone or in combination with one of seven minor subjects (see online for details). The University of Buckingham courses run in nine-week terms and because they are shorter than other universities it offers a wider range of courses. Single Honours psychology students take courses in six of the areas of professional psychology (business, clinical, counselling, educational, forensic and health psychology). Through discounts to fees based on undergraduate performance, strong students are encouraged to stay on for a further year and study for a research master's.

BUCKINGHAMSHIRE NEW

Buckinghamshire New University
High Wycombe Campus
Queen Alexandra Road
High Wycombe HP11 2IZ
Tel: 01494 522141
www.bucks.ac.uk

There is a variety of both BPS and non-BPS accredited psychology courses available at Buckinghamshire New University. Five of its undergraduate degrees confer eligibility to register for GBC with the BPS. With regard to accredited programmes, students can choose from the generic BSc (Hons) Psychology, or more applied areas such as:

- BSc (Hons) Criminological Psychology
- BSc (Hons) Sport Psychology
- BSc (Hons) Psychology and Criminology
- BSc (Hons) Psychology and Sociology.

These all cover the core syllabus components from the BPS-qualifying exam. In addition, the BSc (Hons) Psychology offers a number of career-based option modules at level three. The dissertation in each of these degree programmes is based upon an empirical investigation. Alternatively, students may be interested in studying psychology and working with people but not necessarily wishing to pursue a career as a psychologist. For these students the BSc (Hons) in Psychosocial Studies may be more ideally suited. This is an applied degree programme incorporating problem-based experiential learning and modules focused specifically on social problems such as disability, homelessness, substance misuse etc. All of the degrees have a three-year duration and the teaching is delivered via four year-long modules per year. The teaching typically consists of three hours' taught time per module per week. Each module is delivered so as to include the development of transferable skills and to enhance the employability of graduates. The university has strong links with the local community and the students are encouraged to actively engage in a range of extra-curricular activities.

CAMBRIDGE

Cambridge Admissions Office
Fitzwilliam House
32 Trumpington Street
Cambridge CB2 1QY
Tel: 01223 333308
www.psychol.cam.ac.uk and www.ppsis.cam.ac.uk

Psychology is part of the BA in Natural Sciences or the BA in Politics, Psychology and Sociology (PPS). The Natural Sciences course is based on general scientific training and allows you to study experimental psychology along with other scientific subjects and to specialise in it in the final year. There is the opportunity to work with leading scientists and within the Medical Research Council's Cognition and Brain Sciences Unit, a leading laboratory in psychology research. Competition for places is tough! Psychology is also a pathway within the PPS course at Cambridge. Here psychology is studied alongside politics and sociology in the first year, after which you can choose to focus on psychology in the second and third years. During their final year many students participate in research projects directed by the leading researchers and are thus prepared for careers in research and academia.

Students who take the requisite scheme of study in psychology as part of natural sciences or PPS are normally eligible for admission to professional courses in clinical and educational psychology through graduate membership of the BPS.

CANTERBURY CHRIST CHURCH

Canterbury Christ Church University College
North Holmes Road
Canterbury CT1 1QU
Tel: 01227 782659
www.canterbury.ac.uk/psychology

Psychology is located 'in new facilities' the Department of Applied Social Sciences and may be studied as a Single Honours programme, or in combination with a range of other subjects in the Combined Honours scheme. The undergraduate syllabus is taught using a modular framework and covers areas such as:

- cognitive science
- health psychology
- psychology in education
- social psychology
- therapeutic processes.

The course is well suited to students intending to pursue a career in psychology, as well as those seeking employment in other areas requiring psychological knowledge and skills. Both the Single Honours programme and the major route through the Combined Honours scheme are accredited by the BPS as conferring eligibility for graduate membership (GBC).

CARDIFF

Cardiff University
Cardiff CF10 3XQ
Tel: 029 2087 4000
www.cardiff.ac.uk/psych

The Cardiff School of Psychology is one of the largest psychology departments in the UK. It was rated as 'Excellent' in the most recent TQA, and has the greatest research power of any psychology department in the UK, according to the 2008 RAE. The school offers a three-year BSc (Hons) Psychology degree, and a four-year BSc (Hons) Psychology with Professional Placement degree. Both courses are accredited by the BPS as conferring eligibility for graduate membership with GBC. The modules studied on the two degree schemes are the same, but the four-year course includes a year allowing students to gain experience of psychology in a professional setting between the second and final year. Students take up a wide range of placements covering areas such as clinical psychology, forensic psychology, occupational and work psychology, and research settings.

Placement positions are mainly chosen from among a large menu of possibilities that the school provides, but can also be tailor made for the individual where there is a specific ambition. Teaching includes formal lectures combined with practical classes, computer workshops, video demonstrations and small-group tutorial work. Students receive a sound foundation in psychology with the opportunity to focus on their own interests in the final year. Excellent computing and laboratory facilities support the teaching and staff research activities which include:

- developmental psychology
- face recognition
- family relationships
- health psychology
- motion perception

- neuroscience and neuropsychology
- the effects of drugs on behaviour.

The School of Psychology is also associated with the Cardiff University Brain Research Imaging Centre, which provides state of the art brain imaging facilities.

CHESTER

University of Chester
Parkgate Road
Chester CH1 4BJ
Tel: 01244 513479
www.chester.ac.uk/psychology

Chester offers psychology in Single and Combined Honours degrees, the latter with a wide range of subject combinations in arts, humanities, science and health. The degrees are modular and single and particular routes in Combined Honours degrees are accredited by the BPS as conferring eligibility for graduate membership with GBC. Core modules are undertaken over all three years and the Single Honours degree offers a wide choice of optional modules. Stress is placed on practical work and research methods, and many modules have an applied slant, for example looking at the contribution of psychology to real-world problems, through developmental, organisational and forensic psychology.

CITY

City University
Northampton Square
London EC1V 0HB
Tel: 020 7040 5060
www.city.ac.uk/psychology

The Department of Psychology, which is within the School of Social Sciences, offers a Single Honours degree in Psychology. Psychology does not contribute to any Joint Honours degrees within the school. In the first year students take introductory courses in a range of areas in psychology, as well as one elective module from outside psychology. The second year provides a thorough grounding in the principal areas of psychology, and the third year offers a range of elective modules from both theoretical and applied areas of psychology. The degree is accredited by the BPS as conferring eligibility for graduate membership with GBC.

COVENTRY

Coventry University
Priory Street

Coventry CV1 5FB
Tel: 024 7688 7688
www.coventry.ac.uk/psychology

Three degrees are offered: Psychology, Psychology and Criminology, and Sport Psychology, all of which are accredited by the BPS. These share the common core areas of BPS-recognised degrees as well as a module from the CU Add+vantage scheme and a skills module designed to enhance employability. Psychology at Coventry University covers a broad range of specialist and applied areas, including gender and culture, anomalous experience, psychopathology, forensic and health psychology. The department has a strong research profile, and actively encourages student research to conference and publication level. While the BSc (Hons) Sport Psychology is the first stage towards qualification as a sport psychologist, all three undergraduate course share a common core, permitting graduates to choose from a range of professional careers, and many graduates progress to the health or forensic MSc programmes. The department emphasises career development and the varied and innovative teaching, learning and assessment methods develop a wide range of transferable skills highly valued by employers. The student-centred approach to learning is supported by a strong tutorial system and by CUOnline – an interactive learning environment. A Graduate Certificate and a Graduate Diploma (BPS accredited) are also offered for students, including international students, who wish to have GBC, but have little or no psychology from their previous programme.

DE MONTFORT

De Montfort University
The Gateway
Leicester LE1 9BH
Tel: 0116 255 1551
www.dmu.ac.uk/Subjects/Db/coursePage2.php?courseID=1164

De Montfort University offers three Single Honours programmes:

1| BSc (Hons) in Psychology
2| BSc (Hons) Psychology with Applied Criminology
3| BSc (Hons) Psychology with Health Studies.

All three programmes are accredited as conferring eligibility for the GBC, provided the minimum standard of a Second Class Honours is achieved. This is the first step towards becoming a chartered psychologist. The university also offers six Joint Honours programmes linking psychology with:

1| education studies
2| forensic science
3| health studies

4| human resources
5| law or
6| marketing.

All programmes are supported by staff who are active in their own research areas. An excellent range of facilities are available, including well-equipped research rooms.

The course content adheres to the high standards demand by the BPS, supplementing this core with some exciting modules looking specifically at empirical research and at applied aspects of psychology. One particular element that sets the programme apart is the wide range of options available in year three. Students can select four optional modules from a range of 15 representing different careers in psychology or relating to the research interest of staff.

DERBY

University of Derby
Kedleston Road
Derby DE22 1GB
Tel: 01332 590500
www.derby.ac.uk

Derby offers a BSc Psychology degree, a BSc in Counselling Psychology, and psychology pathways within the university's Joint Honours scheme taught on the Derby campus. All can be taken full or part time. A four-year online distance learning BSc Psychology is also available.

The on-campus and online BSc Psychology degrees and BSc Counselling Psychology are all accredited by the BPS as providing eligibility for graduate membership with GBC. Students who take psychology as part of a Joint Honours degree are also eligible for GBC, provided they take psychology as a major or joint subject.

Courses are offered on a modular basis, and a variety of assessment methods are used, matched to the content of the module. Psychology teaching covers the main theories and methods of contemporary psychology. Many modules include some practical work.

DUNDEE

The University
Dundee DD1 4HN
Tel: 01382 223181
www.dundee.ac.uk/psychology

Psychology may be taken in:

- the Faculty of Arts and Social Sciences
- the Faculty of Science
- the Faculty of Life Sciences
- the Faculty of Engineering and Physical Sciences.

Most psychology teaching is devoted to courses leading to Honours degrees (four years) and general degrees (three years). The course reflects the research interests of the teaching staff but there is an over-riding commitment to present a balanced view of the subject. It is accredited by the BPS as conferring eligibility for graduate membership with GBC. Laboratory work and experience with computers form an integral part of the practical training.

DURHAM

University of Durham
Department of Psychology
Science Laboratories
South Road
Durham DH1 3LE
Tel: 0191 334 3240
www.dur.ac.uk/psychology

The Department of Psychology offers Single Honours degrees in psy-chology as well as participating in natural science, Combined Honours and Joint Honours degrees. The department also offers a BSc Honours degree in Applied Psychology at its Stockton campus. The courses cover a broad range of topics from biological psychology to social psy-chology, and are accredited by the BPS as conferring eligibility for grad-uate membership with GBC. Members of staff are active in all research fields of psychology, with strengths in cognitive psychology, develop-mental psychology and neuroscience.

EAST LONDON

University of East London
Romford Road
London E15 4LZ
Tel: 020 8590 7722
www.uel.ac.uk/psychology

Available full-time and part-time and in both the day and evening, the BSc course (BPS accredited) offers a wide choice of specialist study, including:

- animal behaviour
- cognitive neuropsychology

- counselling
- developing minds
- drugs and behaviour
- evolutionary psychology
- forensic psychology
- occupational psychology
- psychology of mental health.

The department also offers postgraduate research courses in all the main areas of professional applied psychology, as well as having numerous postgraduate research students. A Graduate Diploma course is also offered for graduates of other disciplines who wish to convert their first degree to one which is acceptable for registration with the BPS.

EDGE HILL

Edge Hill University
St Helens Road
Ormskirk L39 4QP
Tel: 01695 575171
www.edgehill.ac.uk/Faculties/HMSAS/DSAPS

The course leads to a BSc Single Honours degree in Psychology and is accredited by the BPS as conferring eligibility for graduate membership with GBC. The three-year full-time programme covers all of the major areas that feature in the BPS qualifying examination:

- biological psychology
- cognitive psychology
- developmental psychology
- personality and individual differences
- research methods
- social psychology.

In the third year a number of specialist options are available, including work psychology, educational psychology, addiction studies, mental health, and the psychology of personal relationships. Students also undertake a supervised research project in their final year. The courses offered are as follows:

- BSc (Hons) Psychology
- BSc (Hons) Educational Psychology
- BSc (Hons) Sports and Exercise Psychology
- BSc (Hons) Health Psychology.

The entry requirements of 240 UCAS points are the same for each course. The Educational Psychology and Health Psychology degrees also include work-based placements.

Psychology was rated 'Excellent' for its teaching by HEFCE in its most recent inspection. The course is taught in purpose-built psychology laboratories. A range of facilities is available, including internet and CD-ROM systems, for example online journals and abstract databases.

EDINBURGH

College of Humanities and Social Sciences (HSS)
Undergraduate Admissions Office
University of Edinburgh
David Hume Tower
George Square
Edinburgh EH8 9JX
Tel: 0131 650 3565
www.psy.ed.ac.uk

The undergraduate programme in psychology at the University of Edinburgh is a four-year course leading either to an MA or to a BSc. The degree courses are accredited by the BPS and, in addition to covering the BPS 'core criteria', Edinburgh has particular strengths in the psychology of language and cognition, health and individual differences, and is currently expanding as a Centre of Excellence in human cognitive neuroscience.

The first-year course assumes no previous experience of psychology, and introduces students to the breadth of the discipline, including biological, cognitive, developmental and social psychology, plus the psychology of individual differences and perception. Second- and third-year courses extend these topics into intermediate and advanced levels. Fourth-year students choose from a broader range of options related to contemporary research issues. Also in the fourth year, students carry out an original research project under staff supervision. Through their choice of options and project work, students have the opportunity to focus on areas in which they are particularly interested. A practical component runs through all four years, which gives training in research methods and statistics.

The university also offers joint degrees that combine psychology with other subjects within the School of Philosophy, Psychology and Language Science, as well as a BSc in Biological Sciences in which psychology can form a part.

EDINBURGH NAPIER

Craglockhart Campus
Edinburgh Napier University
Edinburgh EH14 1DJ
Tel: 08452 606040
www.courses.napier.ac.uk

The course is accredited by the BPS as conferring eligibility for the GBC. In the first year you will study psychology, sociology, effective learning, social psychology, individual differences, and social science research. In the second year you will follow courses in quantitative research, psychology of language and thinking, biological foundations of behaviour, child development, introduction to sport and exercise psychology, animal behaviour, and researching psychology. In the third year you will study lifespan development, social psychology, cognitive neuroscience, and individual differences. You will also undertake some practical work and work on two option topics.

ESSEX

University of Essex
Wivenhoe Park
Colchester CO4 3SQ
Tel: 01206 873333
www.essex.ac.uk/psychology

The Psychology Department at Essex is young, dynamic, enthusiastic and research-orientated. In its own purpose-designed building, the department has the latest facilities for lecture and laboratory-based learning. The degrees at Essex cover the fundamentals of psychology while at the same time providing courses in the most interesting current research topics within a structure designed to maximise student choice. Both the BA and BSc Psychology degrees offered by the University of Essex are fully accredited by the BPS. The degree schemes are identical and cover core areas in psychology, including:

- developmental psychology
- health psychology
- intelligence
- language
- memory
- perception
- research methods
- social psychology
- statistics.

Other degrees which may be of interest are BSc Social Psychology and Sociology and BA Criminology with Social Psychology.

EXETER

University of Exeter
Northcote House
The Queen's Drive

Exeter EX4 4QJ
Tel: 01392 724634
www.exeter.ac.uk/psychology

Psychology is offered as both a BSc and a BA three-year programme and both are identical in content; psychology is taught as a science throughout. Psychology can also be combined with Sport and Exercise Science as a Single Honours BSc and many other subjects through the Flexible Combined Honours programme. All Single Honours programmes are accredited by the BPS as conferring eligibility for graduate membership. The school provides an excellent teaching experience, access to extensive specialist facilities and is recognised as one of the UK's top 10 psychology departments in both *The Times Good University Guide 2010* and the NSS (2009). Exeter is a research-intensive university and is 11th in the UK for world-leading research in psychology (RAE 2008).

GLAMORGAN

University of Glamorgan
Pontypridd CF37 1DL
Tel: 01443 480480
www.glam.ac.uk/hass

The University of Glamorgan offers a number of options for studying psychology as part of an undergraduate programme. The following degrees are accredited by the BPS as conferring eligibility for graduate membership with GBC:

- BSc (Hons) Psychology – Single Honours
- BSc (Hons) Psychology – major award (which allows students to combine psychology with a wide range of other subjects, including criminology, sociology, philosophy, English, history, business studies and marketing)
- BSc (Hons) Developmental Psychology
- BSc (Hons) Sport Psychology.

The above programmes cover the core areas of psychology as stipulated by the BPS but also allow for students to select modules in a number of interesting specialist areas at level three, depending upon their specific programme. Other relevant non-GBC options include BSc (Hons) in Early Years Development and Education and a range of options from the Joint Honours and minor programme. High-quality teaching is supported by a strong research culture. Academic staff are actively involved in a range of research projects which complement their teaching specialisms. These include projects undertaken by members of the Centre for Lifespan Research (launched in September 2005) as well as a number of applied research projects in the fields of sports and health psychology. Staff are also responsible for the delivery of a number of short training courses to business and research-based consultancies. This further informs the teaching on undergraduate programmes and provides students with the opportunity to see how psychology may be applied in the wider world.

GLASGOW

University of Glasgow
Glasgow G12 8QQ
Tel: 0141 330 5089
www.psy.gla.ac.uk

Psychology is a scientific subject with an emphasis on how the brain controls behaviour and experience. Psychology is offered in the faculties of Arts (MA), Science (BSc) and Social Sciences (MA SocSci), the faculty being determined by the subjects that students choose to combine with psychology. The Honours course is taken over four years and can be either Single Honours or Joint Honours, with a variety of combinations possible. Both the Single and Joint Honours courses are accredited by the BPS as conferring eligibility for graduate membership. It is possible for some students to take the third year of the course at an approved university in the USA, Canada or Australia. All core areas of psychology are covered, as well as other topic areas which reflect the broad range of expertise and research areas of the staff. In the final year students carry out an independent research project. Emphasis is placed on employability in the Honours course. The department has a very strong research record in various areas, including perception, neuroscience, addictions, language and cognitive science. It has an excellent track record in TQA and RAE and consistently rates very highly in the NSS.

GLASGOW CALEDONIAN

Glasgow Caledonian University
Cowcaddens Road
Glasgow G4 0BA
Tel: 0141 331 3000
www.gcal.ac.uk/sls/departments/deptofpsychology/

The BSc/BSc (Hons) Psychology programme provides undergraduate education in psychology while allowing students to select modules from complementary non-psychology subject areas including:

- biology
- economics
- European languages

- history
- marketing
- media studies
- politics
- sociology.

In years 3 and 4, students can specialise entirely in psychology or continue to study another subject area if they wish to do so. All students who successfully complete each level of the programme are eligible to proceed to Honours. The Honours programme is accredited by the BPS as conferring eligibility for graduate membership with GBC.

Employability is a key concern of the university and for this reason, a placement option has been introduced. Placements are for a minimum of 30 academic weeks and are available to students who have successfully completed level 3. The placement is not credit-bearing, however, the aim is for participating students to develop their skills and gain work experience either in an applied psychology setting or in relevant employment where knowledge of psychology may be an advantage.

GLOUCESTERSHIRE

Department of Natural and Social Sciences
University of Gloucestershire
Francis Close Hall
Swindon Road
Cheltenham GL50 4AZ
Tel: 01242 714755
www.glos.ac.uk

Psychology is available as a Single Honours BSc or Joint Honours BSc/ BA combining with a wide range of subjects, including biology and criminology. Provided students follow a specified route, both programmes are accredited as conferring eligibility for the GBC with the BPS. Gloucestershire's psychology provision was voted top of all UK institutions for student satisfaction in 2007.

GOLDSMITHS

Goldsmiths College
University of London
London SE14 6NW
Tel: 020 7919 7171
www.goldsmiths.ac.uk/psychology

This is a three-year course in which the final year offers a higher level of specialisation in selected topics including occupational psychology,

cognitive psychology, neuropsychology, social psychology, psychopharmacology, psychology of consciousness and psychopathology. Opportunities for part-time study and intercalated work programmes are
available within the BSc programme. The course is accredited by
the BPS.

GREENWICH

University of Greenwich
School of Health and Social Care
Avery Hill Campus
Avery Hill Road
London SE9 2UG
Tel: 020 8331 7642
www.gre.ac.uk/schools/health

Psychology can be studied as a Single Honours subject (BSc Psychology) or as a major with a minor in Counselling (BSc Psychology with
Counselling). The BSc Psychology degree is accredited by the BPS as
conferring eligibility for graduate membership with GBC. The first year
of study comprises two core courses in psychology alongside courses
chosen from options in other disciplines (including counselling). In the
second year, students cover a core curriculum in psychology which lays
the foundations for more advanced work in the final year, comprising an
independent research project and a variety of specialist courses in
psychology and counselling.

HERTFORDSHIRE

University of Hertfordshire
Hatfield AL10 9AB
Tel: 01707 284000
www.herts.ac.uk/courses/schools-of-study/psychology/home.cfm

The first year of the BSc (Hons) Psychology course lays a strong foundation in core areas of empirical psychology. Modules in applied developmental and social psychology in the second year underpin a choice of
final-year option courses. In the final year, students carry out an independent research project under the supervision of an experienced
researcher. There is an optional short work placement. The BSc (Hons)
Cognitive Science and the BSc (Hons) Psychology with Artificial Intelligence degrees offer students the opportunity to study psychology,
computer programming, philosophy, linguistics and neuroscience in an
integrated programme that addresses questions of human and machine
intelligence. The BSc Psychology and the BSc Psychology with AI both
hold BPS accreditation.

HUDDERSFIELD

University of Huddersfield
Queensgate
Huddersfield HD1 3DH
Tel: 01484 422288
www2.hud.ac.uk/hhs/dbs/psy/index.php

The university offers four BSc courses accredited by the BPS as conferring eligibility for the GBC:

1| Psychology
2| Psychology with Criminology
3| Psychology with Counselling
4| Sport and Exercise Psychology.

All of these degrees provide high-quality, broad-based education in psychology, or psychology with an allied discipline. Each course provides a sound basis of professional training in psychology as well as enabling students to develop interests in related areas. Shared, core modules comprise introductory modules in psychology and research methods, together with foundation modules in the allied discipline, where a student is taking a combined course. The second year builds on the first year with more advanced modules, while in the third and final year students have the opportunity to take specialist modules in psychology, allied areas and a research project.

Other courses in psychology offered, that do not lead to the GBC award, allow students to study psychology in a broader context. These include BA (Hons) Business and Psychology and BSc(Hons) Psychological Studies, offered at the university centres. The distinct nature of all of the psychology courses at the University of Huddersfield lies in their applied nature. Students are therefore encouraged to consider how the theories constructed by psychologists may be applied to real-world issues, and to critically evaluate the implications of such applications.

HULL

University of Hull
Hull HU6 7RX
Tel: 01482 465388
www.hull.ac.uk/05/departments/appsci/psy

This is a three-year BSc in Psychology that is organised so that in the first year students receive a broad introduction to psychology, and in subsequent years modules become more specialised and advanced. Hull also offers a three-year Psychology with Counselling Psychology course and Joint Honours degrees combining Psychology, Sociology,

Philosophy, Criminology and Sports Science. These joint courses last for three years and students spend approximately 70% of their time on psychology components and 30% on their other subject. There is the opportunity for direct entry to postgraduate clinical psychology training from the psychology courses. The course is BPS accredited.

KEELE

The University
Keele ST5 5BG
Tel: 01782 621111
www.keele.ac.uk/depts/ps

Students combine psychology with another subject, following a Joint Honours degree programme which leads to accreditation by the BPS. In addition, first-year students take a one-year course in Complementary Studies which is designed to introduce a third discipline area and develop their academic skills. Over 30 combinations are available with psychology in a Joint Honours programme, including disciplines from the humanities, the social sciences and the natural sciences. Criminology is the most popular subject followed by English, biology, sociology and neuroscience. A modular scheme is followed in which all students take two psychology modules per semester. Students can spend a semester at one of Keele's North American partner institutions during their second year. The school has particular strength in social research, cognition and neuropsychology, and applied psychology.

KENT

University of Kent at Canterbury
Kent CT2 7NZ
Tel: 01227 764000
www.kent.ac.uk/psychology

The department was rated 8th in the country in the *Guardian 2009 University Guide*. It was graded 4 in its last national RAE, with the social psychology research group graded as 5*, the highest grade available. All programmes are accredited by the BPS as conferring eligibility for graduate membership of the Society with GBC, provided students achieve the minimum standard of qualification of Second Class Honours. Kent offers degrees in:

- psychology
- psychology with clinical psychology
- social psychology
- social psychology with clinical psychology
- applied psychology
- applied psychology with clinical psychology

- applied social psychology
- applied social psychology with clinical psychology
- computing and psychology
- psychology and sociology
- psychology and social anthropology
- psychology and law
- European social psychology
- psychology with studies in Europe.

There is the opportunity to spend a year at a European university under the two European programmes. Four-year degrees include a placement where students undertake special project work in the NHS, the prison service or a government research establishment. In the final year, students are able to choose from a range of specialist options, including cognitive, developmental, forensic, health and social psychology.

KINGSTON

Kingston University
Penrhyn Road
Kingston upon Thames KT1 2EE
Tel: 020 8547 2000
www.kingston.ac.uk/psychologybsc/

Psychology is offered under a modular framework giving students considerable autonomy. Tutors are drawn from different faculties. The full BSc Honours degree in Psychology and the major psychology route are accredited by BPS and the half-field route confers eligibility for graduate membership with GBC.

LANCASTER

Lancaster University
University House
Lancaster LA1 4YW
Tel: 01524 593698
www.psych.lancs.ac.uk

In the first year, students spend two-thirds of their time studying psychology and they take one non-psychology course. Psychology then becomes the focus in the second and third years. Students are able to choose whether to graduate with a BA or a BSc, and the course is BPS-registered. There is also a variety of combined degrees, the most popular of which are those with languages. Those combining psychology with a foreign language do a four-year course with one year spent abroad.

LEEDS

Department of Psychology
University of Leeds
Leeds LS2 9JT
Tel: 0113 343 5724
www.psyc.leeds.ac.uk

The Department of Psychology is centrally located on the university precinct. Excellent facilities are provided for both teaching and research. The department received an Excellent in the 2008 RAE. There are approximately 80 staff members, 50 postgraduate students and 770 undergraduate students (550 Single Honours and 220 Joint Honours), with a broad selection of undergraduate and postgraduate psychology courses, which are accredited by the BPS as conferring eligibility for graduate membership with GBC. Research for the department is grouped into three main areas:

1| biological psychology
2| cognitive psychology
3| health and social psychology.

LEEDS TRINITY

Leeds Trinity University College
Horsforth
Leeds LS18 5HD
Tel: 0113 283 7123
www.tasc.ac.uk/depart/psych

Psychology and forensic psychology are studied as a Single Honours subject or in combination with marketing, management, media, human resource management, public relations, journalism, sports and exercise, nutrition and health or sociology (either as a Joint Honours degree or major/minor combination). Both Single and Combined Honours courses are accredited by the BPS as conferring eligibility for graduate membership with GBC. The Department of Psychology has a range of dedicated laboratories and interview/observation suites. In the final year, students have the opportunity to apply their skills and knowledge by conducting an individual research project. Specialised options include: mental health and counselling psychology; health psychology; occupational psychology; forensic psychology and child psychology.

LEICESTER

University of Leicester
University Road

Leicester LE1 7RH
Tel: 0116 252 2522
www.le.ac.uk/psychology

The headquarters of the BPS is situated in Leicester and maintains close links with the department. The research and teaching facilities include two large computer laboratories, a video laboratory, a psychometric test library and a music research library. Research strengths are concentrated in:

- clinical psychology
- cognitive psychology
- development
- forensic psychology
- neuroscience
- occupational psychology
- social behaviour.

BScs are also available in psychology with a designated subsidiary subject. At present these are degrees in psychology with sociology, biology and neuroscience. All degrees offered have graduate recognition status from the BPS.

LINCOLN

University of Lincoln
Brayford Pool
Lincoln LN6 7TS
Tel: 01522 882000
www.lincoln.ac.uk/psychology

There are three psychology programmes – two Single Honours programmes (psychology, and psychology with clinical psychology) and the psychology major programme. The psychology with clinical psychology programme follows the Single Honours psychology degree programme with additional compulsory units in clinical psychology at all three levels. The psychology major is the programme followed by joint students. Psychology can be studied in combination with a wide range of subjects, including criminology, management, health studies and social policy. All three programmes cover the core areas of psychology, supported by units on research methods, information technology, statistics and data analysis. In the final year of the psychology Single Honours programme, students have a wide range of specialist topics to choose from. The programmes are accredited by the BPS.

LIVERPOOL

University of Liverpool
Eleanor Rathbone Building

Bedford Street South
Liverpool L69 7ZA
Tel: 0151 794 2957
www.liv.ac.uk/psychology

There is one psychology programme – the BSc (Hons) in Psychology – with 170 places. The course has at its core the main fields and methods in psychology and is accredited by the BPS as conferring eligibility for graduate membership with GBC. The department has undergone considerable expansion in the last three years. A virtual doubling of staff numbers allows tuition not only through lectures and tutorials but also via interactive experimental work, mainly in individual and small-group projects.

LIVERPOOL HOPE

Liverpool Hope University College
Hope Park
Liverpool L16 9JD
Tel: 0151 291 3000
www.hope.ac.uk/undergraduate-2010/psychology.html

An accredited BPS programme, psychology is offered within the BA/BSc combined modular degree. A wide variety of final-year options is offered, including cognitive psychology, educational psychology, developmental psychology and parapsychology. Facilities within the department include different labs, such as cognition labs, a perception lab and an observation lab. Liverpool Hope University defines itself as a teaching-led and research-informed university. The university has the commitment to provide a quality learning experience. Practical work is as much as possible interlinked with ongoing research projects.

LIVERPOOL JOHN MOORES

Liverpool John Moores University
Roscoe Court
4 Rodney Street
Liverpool L1 2TZ
Tel: 0151 2313 313
www.ljmu.ac.uk/psychology

Four distinctive Single Honours BSc programmes are offered – applied psychology, psychology and biology, psychology and forensic science, and forensic psychology and criminal justice. In addition, psychology is offered in a joint or major/minor programme with criminology. Single Honours programmes and degrees with psychology as a major subject are accredited by the BPS as conferring eligibility for graduate membership with GBC.

LONDON MET

Department of Psychology
London Metropolitan University
City Campus
Calcutta House
Old Castle Street
London E1 7NT
Tel: 020 7320 1067
www.londonmet.ac.uk

The Department of Psychology has been offering degrees in psychology for over 35 years. The department has two locations; City Campus is located in Calcutta House at the edge of the City of London and North Campus is located in Ladbroke House close to Highbury, north London. City Campus currently offers a broad-based BSc Psychology degree which is accredited by the BPS as conferring eligibility for graduate membership with GBC.

Level 1 provides a foundation in the core areas of psychology: cognitive, developmental and social psychology, individual differences, biological psychology and research methods. Level 2 builds on these foundations in greater depth to provide a grounding in these core areas. Some level 1 modules also provide general support for the transition to higher education as well as teaching skills and techniques that are specific to the discipline of psychology. Experimental work at level 1 is conducted in a class context and at level 2 in small groups. At level 3 students undertake an independent research project and select specialist options from a broad range of choices, including abnormal psychology, atypical development, environmental psychology, and cross-cultural psychology, as well as advanced options in cognitive, social, biological and developmental psychology. Students also have the opportunity to select more vocationally oriented options, such as forensic, health and occupational psychology, which reflect the extensive portfolio of professional expertise and postgraduate courses available at City Campus.

The department also offers the BSc Applied Psychology degree at North Campus. However, this does not confer the GBC with the BPS, but is suitable for applicants who do not wish to pursue a career as a professional psychologist.

LONDON SOUTH BANK

London South Bank University
90 London Road
London SE1 6LN
Tel: 020 7815 7815
www.lsbu.ac.uk/psycho

The Psychology Department offers flexible Single Honours courses in psychology. In addition to the Single Honours course, there is also a choice of pathways in psychology with clinical psychology, or psychology with child development. Students can also major in psychology and minor in criminology. The department has three research groupings – cognition in health behaviours, memory in applied settings, and developmental disorders. The department ranked highly amongst London post-92 universities in the last RAE. The department has recently upgraded laboratory facilities for student use, now including state-of-the art eye-tracking equipment. In addition, there is a highly successful work placement scheme which assists students into psychology-relevant voluntary work experience in clinical, developmental and occupational settings. All of the undergraduate courses are BPS-accredited.

LOUGHBOROUGH

Loughborough University
Loughborough LE11 3TU
Tel: 01509 263171
www.lboro.ac.uk/departments/hu; www.lboro.ac.uk/departments/ss

There are two distinct psychology programmes offered at Loughborough University – human psychology and social psychology.

Human psychology

The Human Psychology Department offers multi-disciplinary study in biology, ergonomics, psychology and psychology with ergonomics. An important feature of the psychology programme is its situation within this well-established multidisciplinary department. Research and teaching are both highly respected – *The Times Good University Guide 2010* rated the school 8th for psychology. Both the Psychology and Psychology with Ergonomics degrees are accredited by the BPS as conferring eligibility for graduate membership with GBC, whilst the Psychology with Ergonomics degree is also recognised for professional membership of the Ergonomics Society. The relationship between theory and application is a concern that runs through all the programmes. Students are encouraged from the outset to consider the relevance of psychology and to become involved in academic work that informs and develops its critical use and application. To achieve this, the programme is entirely oriented towards the study of human beings. The organisation of the degree content into modular topics also allows the opportunity to participate in subjects elsewhere in the department and university. This allows students to tailor their degree programme to their developing interests and career choices.

Social psychology

The Social Psychology course in the Department of Social Sciences was created in 1974 for students wishing to study psychology from a social rather than a biological perspective. The course covers the main topics of psychology, including laboratory work, and also offers modules in such topics as sexuality, crime, psychopathology and prejudice. Students may take modules from the other disciplines within the department: sociology, media and communications, and social policy. The course is accredited by the BPS as conferring eligibility for graduate membership with GBC. The Department of Social Sciences was ranked 5th in the UK in the 2008 RAE, with 25% of the departments research classed as 'world leading' (rated 4*).

LUTON

University of Luton
Park Square
Luton LU1 3JU
Tel: 01582 734111
www.luton.ac.uk/departments/psychology

The Department of Psychology was established in 1993 and is in the Faculty of Creative Arts, Technology and Sciences. In the ensuing period of rapid growth and high student demand, standards have been externally endorsed as 'Excellent' in the teaching of psychology, with the provision of first-rate accommodation for both teaching and research. The department offers a range of undergraduate BSc (Hons) degree courses in Psychology, Health Psychology, Psychology and Criminology and Applied Psychology. These degree courses are accredited by the BPS and, provided that the prescribed pathways are followed, they confer eligibility for graduate membership with GBC. The department also offers CertHE in Psychology.

MANCHESTER

University of Manchester
Oxford Road
Manchester M13 9PL
Tel: 0161 275 2585
www.psych-sci.manchester.ac.uk

The department was established in 1919 and was the first in Great Britain to appoint a full-time Professor of Psychology. The majority of students work towards a BA or BSc Psychology degree that takes three years to attain. There are no differences between the two courses and the two titles only exist for historical reasons. There is also a joint degree in Psychology and Neuroscience. The neuroscience element covers a range of relevant biological topics as well as neurobiology. Psychology may be studied as an option as part of the BA Combined Studies in Art or BA in Human Communication. The BA and the BSc in Psychology are accredited by the BPS as conferring eligibility for graduate membership with GBC, but the joint degrees in Psychology and Neuroscience, the BA in Human Communication and the BA Combined Studies are not.

MANCHESTER MET

Manchester Metropolitan University
All Saints
Manchester M15 6BH
Tel: 0161 247 2000
www.mmu.ac.uk

The department offers a unique range of courses, providing a comprehensive and integrated study of the fundamental areas of the discipline, and the opportunity to specialise. All courses listed here are accredited by the BPS as conferring eligibility for graduate membership with GBC. There is a Combined Honours degree, allowing psychology to be studied as a major along with a wide range of other subjects, and a four-year degree in Psychology and Speech Pathology, which is recognised also by the Royal College of Speech and Language Therapists, thereby providing graduates with a dual qualification. Opportunities exist for part of the course to be spent elsewhere in Europe, Australia or the USA.

MIDDLESEX

Middlesex University
White Hart Lane
London N17 8HR
Tel: 020 8411 5000
www.mdx.ac.uk/subjects/ss/psy

The psychology degree at Middlesex University was one of the first in the UK to be recognised by the BPS. Formats of study include Single Honours degree, specialised programmes (such as psychology with criminology or psychology, sport and performance), or as a major/minor subject combined with another discipline. By choosing an appropriate mix of core and optional modules students can follow a pathway that not only appeals to their interests but is recognised by the BPS and provides a foundation for the many career choices available within psychology. There is also the opportunity to undertake a sandwich degree which incorporates a work placement, providing students with the opportunity to gain experience in several different areas, including clinical, occupational, forensic, health and educational psychology. Students opting for the sandwich degree also earn a Diploma in Occupational Studies.

MMU CHESHIRE

MMU Cheshire
Department of Interdisciplinary Studies
Crewe CW1 5DU
Tel: 0161 247 2000
www.cheshire.mmu.ac.uk

Psychology is part of the Combined Honours provision at MMU Cheshire. The programme is offered either as a BA or a BSc, and students need to take at least three units per year in psychology. In the final year of this programme, students must undertake an independent project. There is also the opportunity to undertake a programme in the Psychology of Sport and Exercise. This programme is designed to meet the needs of those who intend to pursue a future career in the area, and is a joint venture between the Department of Interdisciplinary Studies and the Department of Exercise and Sport Science. Students study fundamental concepts within psychology with an emphasis on sport and exercise science, and they are encouraged to explore the relationship between theory and practice and to appreciate the application of psychological principles to sport and exercise. Cheshire is currently in the process of seeking BPS accreditation for the Combined Honours course. The BSc in Psychology of Sport and Exercise course is accredited by the BPS as conferring eligibility for graduate membership with GBC.

NEWCASTLE

University of Newcastle upon Tyne
6 Kensington Terrace
Newcastle upon Tyne NE1 7RU
Tel: 0191 222 5594
www.ncl.ac.uk/psychology

The BSc in Psychology at Newcastle is accredited by the BPS. It explores many aspects of psychology, including human and animal behaviour, and provides the flexibility for students to specialise in areas of particular interest. Psychology may also be studied as a Joint Honours degree with Biology, Statistics or Mathematics, or as part of the BA Combined, Studies degree. These are not accredited by the BPS.

Newcastle has strong research areas in fields such as neuroscience, psychiatry and animal behaviour.

NORTHAMPTON

University of Northampton
Boughton Green Road
Northampton NN2 7AL
Tel: 01604 735500
www.northampton.ac.uk/departments/socialsciences/

Students at Northampton can study psychology as a Single Honours subject or as part of a Combined Honours programme which enables them to study psychology as a major, minor or joint subject. Empirical investigation is integral to all the psychology courses, and there is progression through each degree towards specialist final-year options. These include clinical psychology, parapsychology, forensic psychology and neuropsychology. Provided that the specified pathways are followed, the course is accredited by the BPS as conferring eligibility for graduate membership with GBC.

NORTHUMBRIA

University of Northumbria at Newcastle
Ellison Building
Ellison Place
Newcastle upon Tyne NE1 8ST
Tel: 0191 232 6002
http://northumbria.ac.uk/sd/academic/psychsport

The psychology degree has a substantial practical component and includes basic training in research methods, supervised practical classes, training in the use of standardised tests and a substantial final-year research project. It is also possible to study psychology in combination with sport science. All these degrees are accredited by the BPS as conferring eligibility for graduate membership with GBC.

NOTTINGHAM

University of Nottingham
University Park
Nottingham NG7 2RD
Tel: 0115 951 5151
www.psychology.nottingham.ac.uk

The School of Psychology is one of the largest and strongest in the country, with excellent laboratories and IT facilities. There are leading research groups in developmental psychology, cognition and cognitive neuroscience, and computational modelling. The first and second years contain all the compulsory core modules for BPS accreditation, enabling finalists to concentrate on areas of interest. Practical and statistical modules are taken in the first two years to prepare for the third-year project, which accounts for one third of the final-year grade. All students register for a BSc degree, although applicants with arts and humanities A levels, or a mixture, are encouraged to apply. Students take different subsidiary modules in their first year depending on their background. There is a Joint Honours programme with Philosophy and a BSc in Psychology and Cognitive Neuroscience.

NOTTINGHAM TRENT

The Faculty of Economic and Social Science
Nottingham Trent University
Burton Street
Nottingham NG1 4BU
Tel: 0115 848 4060
www.ntu.ac.uk/s3

Psychology with BPS accreditation is offered as a Single Honours BSc degree course and as Combined Honours degrees with either criminology, sociology or sports science. The courses cover a range of approaches to psychology, with an emphasis on behavioural science. The first year provides a strong foundation whilst the following years offer a choice of options and the possibility of specialisation. Research methods, data analysis and application of psychology run throughout all these courses. Students will gain skills in analysis, research, communication and IT. New laboratory facilities and high-quality teaching and support ensure that students have the opportunity to make the most of their time at university.

OXFORD

Admissions Office
Wellington Square
University of Oxford
Oxford OX1 2JD
Tel: 01865 288000
www.psy.ox.ac.uk

You can study psychology at Oxford in two ways: either as a part subject in the Joint Honours school with Philosophy and/or Physiology, or as a subject on its own in Experimental Psychology. Either route is accredited by the BPS as conferring eligibility for graduate membership with GBC. Decisions on selection are made by individual colleges, not by the Department of Experimental Psychology. You should choose a college which has a tutor in psychology (not available at Exeter, Keble, Lincoln, Mansfield, Merton, St Peter's or Trinity). The first two terms consist of three introductory courses. You will then be examined at the end of your second term (an examination called Prelims), which allows you to move on to Part 1 (core courses) and Part 2 (options) of the Final Honours School.

OXFORD BROOKES

Oxford Brookes University
Gipsy Lane
Oxford OX3 0BP
Tel: 01865 484848
www.brookes.ac.uk/undergraduate/courses/psych

Within the School of Social Sciences and Law, Psychology is a three-year BA/BSc course studied either as a Single Honours degree or as a joint degree with one from over 60 other subjects from across the university. It is possible to change to a Single Honours course after the first year. The department recently received an 'Excellent' quality assurance rating. The course is modular and emphasises practical and laboratory experience. A range of assessments is used, including seminars, coursework and examinations. With an appropriate course of study, the course is accredited by the BPS as conferring eligibility for graduate membership with GBC. The department also offers a one-year conversion course to the GBC for non-psychology graduates.

PLYMOUTH

University of Plymouth
Drake Circus
Plymouth PL4 8AA
Tel: 01752 600600
www.plymouth.ac.uk/psychology

There are opportunities to study psychology as a single or joint degree and to obtain work experience under two different routes. The first way is through the Visits Programme in which students attend an organisation that does work relevant to psychology. Attendance is for one half-day per week for one semester. This programme is the first of its kind in the UK. The second route is through a sandwich placement year. Successful completion of the year entitles you to the Certificate of Industrial and Professional Experience. Both the Single Honours BSc in Psychology and its Joint Honours programmes (with Criminal Justice, Human Biology, Law and Sociology) are accredited by the BPS as conferring eligibility for graduate membership with GBC.

PORTSMOUTH

University of Portsmouth
Winston Churchill Avenue

Portsmouth PO1 2UP
Tel: 023 9284 6313
www.port.ac.uk/departments/academic/psychology

The Department of Psychology offers a Single Honours BSc in Psychology, a Single Honours BSc in Forensic Psychology and several other Honours degrees with psychology as a minor. These degrees are delivered over three years with two semesters per year, but may also be taken on a part-time basis over six years. All are accredited by the BPS as conferring eligibility for graduate membership with GBC. Both BSc courses emphasise a 'hands-on' approach to the subject and encourage links with ongoing staff research. The department has well-equipped laboratory facilities and current research interests include: child witnesses; police interviewing; primate communication; the detection of deception; ecological approaches to intentionality; developmental disorders e.g. autism; the origins and development of social cognition and attention and object recognition.

QUEEN MARGARET

Queen Margaret University College
Clerwood Terrace
Edinburgh EH12 8TS
Tel: 0131 317 3000
www.qmuc.ac.uk/psych

Psychology degrees are offered over three or four years; the three-year option provides an ordinary degree and the four-year option provides a BSc (Hons) either in Psychology or in Health Psychology. It is also possible to include psychology as part of the joint degrees scheme, either as a major, joint or minor subject, for example with sociology and social policy, or business and marketing. Success at Honours level in any of these awards confers eligibility for graduate membership of the BPS with GBC. Health psychology is a particular speciality at QMUC, although staff have a wide variety of interests.

QUEEN'S BELFAST

Queen's University of Belfast
University Road
Belfast BT7 1NN
Tel: 028 902 45133
www.psych.qub.ac.uk

The subject review of psychology rated the teaching quality of psychology at Queen's as 'Excellent', awarding a maximum score of 24. Students follow a three-year degree programme leading to an Honours degree in Psychology (accredited by the BPS). The school has extensive computing facilities for students. It has specialised teaching facilities for cognitive, perception, social, developmental, psychobiological, and sport and exercise psychology, and animal behaviour. The school has close links with local hospitals and schools where many students undertake projects. The school offers opportunities to study a wide variety of topics covering the breadth of the discipline.

READING

Department of Psychology
School of Psychology and Clinical Language Sciences
University of Reading
Harry Pitt Building
Earley Gate
Reading RG6 6AL
Tel: 0118 378 8523
www.reading.ac.uk/psychology

The Department of Psychology in the School of Psychology and Clinical Language Science offers Single Honours BSc degrees in: Psychology; Psychology, Childhood and Ageing; and Psychology, Mental and Physical Health. Psychology may also be combined with philosophy, art, biology or mathematics. All these degree programmes are accredited by the BPS as conferring eligibility for graduate membership with GBC.

ROEHAMPTON

Roehampton University
Whitelands College
Holybourne Avenue
London SW15 4JD
Tel: 020 8392 3619/3278
www.roehampton.ac.uk

Psychology is a well-established and expanding subject area within the School of Human and Life Sciences at Roehampton. The department is located at Whitelands College, which offers excellent research and teaching facilities in a state-of-the-art building. The undergraduate programmes are all accredited by the BPS as conferring eligibility for graduate membership with GBC. Students can register for Single or Combined Honours Psychology programmes, or for Psychology and Counselling. All programmes offer a diversity of topics and methods that reflect the interests and expertise of the teaching team and contemporary developments in the discipline as a whole.

ROYAL HOLLOWAY

Royal Holloway
University of London
Egham Hill
Egham TW20 0EX
Tel: 01784 434455
www.rhul.ac.uk/Psychology

The Psychology Department has links with hospitals, schools and businesses, which can be especially useful for the experimental project carried out in the second and third years. There is a newly built teaching laboratory and good facilities, including a state-of-the-art MRI scanner (which cost over £1,000,000), physiological recording equipment, and closed circuit TV and radio. The Single Honours BSc Psychology is accredited by the BPS as conferring eligibility for graduate membership with GBC. At third-year level, students have a wide choice of courses, all of which are taught by leading experts in their respective areas.

ST ANDREWS

University of St Andrews
College Gate
St Andrews KY16 9AJ
Tel: 01334 476161
http://psy.st-andrews.ac.uk

Psychology can be taken in either the Arts Faculty (resulting in the award of an MA) or the Science Faculty (resulting in the award of a BSc) within the four-year structure of Scottish degrees. The psychology components of the degrees in arts and science do not differ. The first two years allow students to take additional subjects which interest them and which may be quite independent of their study of psychology. After two years, students who have done well can elect to take the Honours Psychology degree either as Single Honours or as Joint Honours with any of a number of other subjects. The Single Honours course has full BPS accreditation; the Joint Honours may also be accredited, depending on the components of the psychology course taken.

SHEFFIELD

University of Sheffield
Western Bank
Sheffield S10 2TN
Tel: 0114 222 2000
www.shef.ac.uk/psychology

The Department of Psychology has approximately 400 undergraduate students on three-year psychology courses with BPS accreditation. Special strengths of the course are neuroscience, developmental health and social psychology. There are joint courses in psychology and philosophy, as well as postgraduate courses in occupational and clinical psychology. Students come from all over the world with a range of qualifications and backgrounds. The Single Honours degree in Psychology is accredited by the BPS as conferring eligibility for graduate membership with GBC, as are the dual Honours degrees, provided that at least 50% of the course is in psychology and the relevant modules have been taken.

SHEFFIELD HALLAM

Sheffield Hallam University
Howard Street
Sheffield S1 1WB
Tel: 0114 225 5555
www.shu.ac.uk/psychology

Two psychology-related courses are offered – a BSc in Psychology and a BSc in Psychology and Law. Both are accredited by the BPS. The psychology course covers health, developmental, biological, cognitive and social psychology, and gives students scope to specialise through a range of optional modules. In the psychology and law course, the two subjects are initially studied as separate disciplines, but in the final year students concentrate on the links and overlaps between them by studying modules such as the psychology of crime and law, and legal perspectives. The university has research cubicles with facilities including eye-tracking equipment and electroencephalography (EEG) machines, as well as a 70-seater psychology laboratory. The last QAA subject review rated the teaching of psychology as 'Excellent', awarding it a grade of 24.

SOUTHAMPTON

University of Southampton
University Road
Southampton SO17 1BJ
Tel: 023 8059 5000
www.psychology.soton.ac.uk

The School of Psychology is part of the University of Southampton's Faculty of Medicine, Health and Life Sciences. With a student body of nearly 700 students, the school is one of the largest schools in the country. The undergraduate degree programme has been designed to give a thorough insight into many disciplines in psychology, including clinical, health, cognitive, developmental, learning and social. Lectures are given by experts in their fields. In the most recent national RAE (2008), the School of Psychology ranked 8th in the UK. The curriculum covers a wide range of topics to equip graduates for their future careers. The BSc in Psychology is accredited by the BPS as conferring eligibility for graduate membership with GBC. During the BPS accreditation visit in May 2005 the BPS commended the school for its excellent undergraduate programme and resources.

SOUTHAMPTON SOLENT

Southampton Solent University
East Park Terrace
Southampton SO14 0YN
Tel: 023 8031 9000
www.solent.ac.uk/fmas

The School of Human Sciences offers a well established Single Honours degree in Psychology (BSc (Hons) Psychology), which is accredited by the BPS as conferring eligibility for graduate membership with GBC. Four new psychology pathways have recently been validated:

1| BSc (Hons) Psychology (Counselling), BPS accredited
2| BSc (Hons) Psychology (Criminal Behaviour), BPS accredited
3| BSc (Hons) Psychology (Education)
4| BSc (Hons) Psychology (Health Psychology), BPS accredited.

On all of these courses you will study mind and behaviour within the main disciplines of the field (cognitive, developmental, individual differences, psychobiology and social), as well as studying research methodology. A variety of option units is available in the third year, during which students also carry out an individual project. There is an emphasis throughout the course, and especially within the third year, on the application of psychology to 'real-world' issues. Dedicated laboratories and computing resources are available to facilitate practical work. Psychology can also be studied with criminology in two pathways:

1| BA (Hons) Criminology and Psychology
2| BA (Hons) Criminal Investigation with Psychology.

STAFFORDSHIRE

Staffordshire University
College Road
Stoke-on-Trent ST4 2DE
Tel: 01782 294643
www.staffs.ac.uk/schools/sciences/psychology

A Single Honours Psychology programme is offered, as well as a range of other courses including:

- health psychology
- psychology and child development

- psychology and counselling
- psychology and criminology
- psychology and life challenges
- psychology and sociology.

All programmes are accredited by the BPS as conferring eligibility for grad-uate membership with GBC. Psychology at Staffordshire was ranked 4th in the 2008 National Student Survey. The courses offer a very wide range of applied psychology options in the final year of study. Staff are active in research across many different fields of psychology.

STIRLING

The University of Stirling
Stirling FK9 4LA
Tel: 01786 467640
www.psychology.stir.ac.uk

Psychology may either be studied at Stirling as a Single Honours pro-gramme, or be combined with another subject (in all, there's a choice of 15 such Combined Honours programmes). All Single and Combined Honours programmes are accredited by the BPS, so all students have the opportunity of gaining BPS graduate membership with GBC. Students are accepted for entry in either September or February.

At Stirling there is a strong emphasis on research-based teaching and stu-dents can expect instruction in both theoretical and practical-based aspects of the subject. This approach aims not only to provide students with a wide range of theoretical knowledge across all key areas of the subject, but also to equip them with the necessary research skills to allow them to design, conduct and report on their own research projects. In addition, in the final-year electives, students have the chance to explore in detail specialist areas of psychology that may not be encountered as part of the mainstream cur-riculum. Examples of topic choices for elective courses have included:

- community psychology
- evolutionary psychology
- mass human conflict
- music and spirituality
- the systematic study of dreams.

In the most recent TQA the department was rated as 'Excellent'. The Psychology Department at Stirling is renowned for the quality of its innovative and original research and many of the staff are known world-wide for their research outputs.

STRATHCLYDE

University of Strathclyde
Richmond Street

Glasgow G1 1XQ
Tel: 0141 552 4400
www.strath.ac.uk/psychology

In the first year, psychology may be chosen as one of four subjects selected from a range of classes in arts, social sciences and business studies. Students can then choose psychology and one other subject and continue their study in the second and third years. In the fourth year psychology may be studied to Single or Joint Honours levels. Admission to psychology classes in both the second year and the Honours year is selective. The department has particular strengths in the areas of:

- developmental and educational psychology
- interactive learning
- neuropsychology
- occupational and health psychology
- perceptual-motor skills
- psychology and communication and information technology
- psychology of language and human communication
- road-user behaviour
- social psychology.

The BA in Psychology is accredited by the BPS as conferring eligibility for graduate membership with GBC, as is the Joint Honours programme, provided that the student has undertaken the dissertation in psychology.

SUNDERLAND

University of Sunderland
Edinburgh Building
Chester Road
Sunderland SR1 3SD
Tel: 0191 515 3000
www.sunderland.ac.uk

On this programme, students will be introduced to all areas of psychology as well as studying the research methods and statistical analyses that underpin psychological research. As well as this, students will be able to select optional modules from a wide variety of areas, such as evolutionary psychology, psychology of terrorism, sexual behaviour and intimate relationships, and counselling psychology. Both Single and Combined Honours programmes are available, both of which are accredited by the BPS as conferring eligibility for graduate membership in the BPS (although this only applies to combined subjects students who have psychology as their major award).

SURREY

University of Surrey
Guildford GU2 7XH

Tel: 01483 300800
www.surrey.ac.uk/Psychology

This is a four-year course in which the third year is organised around a period of professional placements so that the students have direct experience of the practical applications of psychology. It enables them to bring this experience back to the university and apply it to final-year studies. There are also extensive international links with the United States or, through the Erasmus programme, with France, Italy or Spain. Surrey also offers a four-year BSc in Applied Psychology and Sociology that stresses the integration of theory and practice – whether it be industry, urban development, social welfare, health or education. The BScs in Psychology and in Applied Psychology and Sociology are accredited by the BPS, and the BSc in Psychology also confers eligibility for GBC.

SUSSEX

University of Sussex
Falmer
Brighton BN1 9RH
Tel: 01273 876638
www.sussex.ac.uk/psychology

Sussex offers a single BSc in Psychology, with a unique flexible structure in which students spend 75% of their time studying core psychology courses, and can decide whether to spend the remaining 25% studying further psychology courses, or courses from other disciplines such as sociology, media studies, philosophy and neuroscience. The university also offers a four-year Psychology with American Studies BSc, in which year three is spent studying at a university in North America. All psychology degrees are BPS accredited. The Psychology Department is one of the largest in the country and has excellent research facilities. It is situated centrally at the university's attractive campus, close to the city of Brighton.

SWANSEA

Swansea University
Singleton Park
Swansea SA2 8PP
Tel: 01792 513023
www.swansea.ac.uk/psychology

The Psychology Department was the first to be awarded an 'Excellent' rating by the Higher Education Funding Council for the quality of its teaching environment. Psychology can be studied as a single subject (BSc Single Honours) or one of a pair of subjects (Joint Honours). Joint Honours degree subjects include psychology with one of the following:

- biological sciences (BSc)
- computer science (BSc)
- criminology (BSc)
- economics (BSc)
- English (BA)
- French (BA)
- German (BA)
- Italian (BA)
- law (BSc or LLB)
- Spanish (BA)
- Welsh (BA).

Undergraduate degrees are three years in duration, except for Joint Honours with European Languages, which are four years long, with the third year spent abroad. Both Single Honours and Joint Honours undergraduate degrees are accredited by the BPS and confer GBC, providing the recommended modules are followed, the supervised project module is successfully completed and a minimum of 2:2 is achieved. The department has a strong research record; members of staff are internationally recognised active researchers with an extensive range of research interests.

The department is friendly, well organised, with good student support and excellent teaching facilities. Teaching methods used within the department include lectures; small group-work (tutorials); laboratories; projects; assignments and examinations. In a Government Audit, undergraduate students in the Psychology Department at Swansea University were '. . . more satisfied overall with their psychology course than in any other psychology course in Wales'. The department also offers postgraduate master's and PhD programmes.

TEESSIDE

University of Teesside
Middlesborough TS1 3BA
Tel: 01642 218121
www.tees.ac.uk/schools/sssl/psychology.cfm

The three-year BSc Psychology course places an emphasis on 'hands-on' research experience through laboratory research classes. Core modules include foundations of:

- biopsychology
- cognitive psychology
- developmental psychology
- perception
- psychology
- social psychology.

07 Psychology courses across the UK

All Teesside's psychology courses (including BScs in Forensic Psychology, Health Psychology, Psychology and Counselling, Sport and Exercise Psychology, and Psychology and Criminology) are accredited by the BPS as conferring eligibility for graduate membership with GBC.

THAMES VALLEY

Thames Valley University
St Mary's Road
London W5 5RF
Tel: 0800 036 8888
http://psyche.tvu.ac.uk

The specialist BSc (Hons) Psychology course at Thames Valley University (TVU) is one of the longest-established psychology courses in the UK and is accredited by the BPS as conferring eligibility for graduate membership with GBC. The course includes a placement during which students will have the opportunity to analyse the relationship between psychological theory and practice, and to gain experience of applying psychological understanding in a health, community or research setting. TVU also offers a BA (Hons) in Psychology and a BSc (Hons) in Psychology with Counselling Theory. All of the courses allow students to gain a full grounding and explore the process of psychological research.

UCL

University College London
Gower Street
London WC1E 6BT
Tel: 020 7679 2000
www.psychol.ucl.ac.uk

One of the first British laboratories in experimental psychology was established at UCL in 1897 and it was here in 1901 that the BPS was inaugurated. The Psychology Department is now the largest in the UK and is a major centre for psychological research, with strengths in vision, cognition, neuropsychology and clinical psychology. Its experimental work is supported by three research councils and many other research-oriented bodies. The BSc Single Honours degree in Psychology is accredited by the BPS as conferring eligibility for graduate membership with GBC.

During the first two years, students study all aspects of the subject and take course units outside the department. Laboratory work in the second year involves students designing and conducting their own experiments in small groups, which provides a basis for the final-year project.

In the final year, in addition to the compulsory research project, students may study a variety of courses such as occupational psychology, language and cognition, visual perception, social psychology and theory of mind. All candidates to whom places are offered are interviewed (overseas applicants excepted).

UCLan

University of Central Lancashire
Preston PR1 2HE
Tel: 01772 201201
www.uclan.ac.uk/scitech/psychology

The University of Central Lancashire (UCLan) offers a flexible psychology programme that is accredited by the BPS as conferring eligibility for graduate membership with GBC, provided a minimum standard of Second Class Honours is achieved. There are five routes through the programme leading to a BSc in Psychology. At levels 1 and 2 all students take the same psychology modules plus a free choice 'elective'. At level 2, those wishing to follow a specialist route take an elective in applied psychology, forensic psychology, neuropsychology or sport psychology. At level 3 students take modules appropriate for their chosen route and complete a double-module project on a relevant topic. Psychology may also be studied as a major, joint or minor subject on the Combined Honours programme (for example, psychology and criminology) and the major 'professional route' is recognised by the BPS as conferring eligibility for GBC. The department also offers MSc programmes in forensic psychology and in health psychology that are accredited by the BPS for Part 1 professional training, as well as a master's programme in psychology, developmental psychology and social psychology. For those who already have a degree there is the Graduate Diploma in Psychological Studies (BPS-recognised for GBC).

ULSTER

University of Ulster
Cromore Road
Coleraine BT52 1SA
Tel: 08700 400 700
www.science.ulster.ac.uk/psychology

At its Coleraine campus on the north coast, Ulster offers a BSc (Hons) in Psychology and a BSc in Social Psychology, both with a full one-year placement available on a competitive basis. At the Magee campus in the historic city of Derry, Ulster offers a BSc (Hons) in Psychology. All of Ulster's psychology degrees are accredited by the BPS as conferring eligibility for graduate membership with GBC.

UWIC

University of Wales Institute Cardiff
Llandaff Campus
Western Avenue
Cardiff CF5 2YB
Tel: 029 2041 7011
www.uwic.ac.uk/shss

UWIC offers a full-time, Single Honours psychology degree (BSc Hons Psychology), accredited by the BPS as conferring eligibility for graduate membership with GBC. In the first year, students are introduced to core psychology subjects which are developed over the following two years. In the third year of the course, students have the opportunity to select option modules that reflect their interests in psychology or the careers that they wish to follow. In addition, third-year students undertake their own research on a psychology topic for their undergraduate project. Assessed coursework and examinations take place in all three years. All modules must be passed to gain a degree, but the degree classification depends on the results from the second and third years of the course. The degree is validated by the University of Wales.

WARWICK

University of Warwick
Coventry CV4 7AL
Tel: 02476 523723
www2.warwick.ac.uk/fac/sci/psych

Warwick offers a Single Honours BSc in Psychology which is accredited by the BPS as conferring eligibility for graduate membership with GBC. It is a three-year programme offering a general grounding in methodology and the principal areas of psychology. Thus a quarter of the degree credit comes from practical and project work, with the remainder coming from courses in biological, cognitive, developmental, social and abnormal psychology. The first two years consist of core courses in these areas, enabling the third year to contain a core project and a choice of six options from a list of about 12. Assessment comes from exams (50%), with the remaining 50% coming from essays, project reports, presentations and tests.

WEST OF SCOTLAND

University of the West of Scotland
Tel: 0141 848 3000
www.uws.ac.uk/schoolsdepts/socialsciences/index.asp

In August 2007, University of Paisley and Bell College merged to create Scotland's biggest modern university with campuses in Ayr, Dumfries,

Hamilton and Paisley. Given the new, enhanced regional status of the university, the name has changed to University of the West of Scotland (UWS).

The university offers two main psychology programmes. Each can be taken over three years for a BA/BSc or four years for a BA/BSc (Hons). The programme encourages students to use the findings, theories and methods of psychology to explore and understand life in contemporary society. In the third and fourth years, in addition to the core elements of the programme, you can choose 'elective' modules from psychology or the other science and social science areas. It is also possible to combine psychology with other disciplines (for example politics, sociology). A comprehensive personal tutorial system is offered and courses are geared towards specific careers or postgraduate study. Both the BA (Hons) and the BSc (Hons) Psychology degrees are accredited by the BPS as conferring eligibility for graduate membership with GBC. The joint degrees are not accredited.

WESTMINSTER

University of Westminster
309 Regent Street
London W1B 2UW
Tel: 020 7911 5088
www.westminster.ac.uk

BSc Psychology is a Single Honours degree offered at Regent Campus in central London. The course provides coverage of core areas of the discipline of psychology, while the option modules deal with the application of psychological theory and research, and give insight into the practice of psychology in a range of settings. Core modules such as social psychology, individual differences and developmental psychology are taken within the first and second year. There is a choice of applied areas in the third year including cognitive disorders, forensic psychology, business psychology and health psychology. The course can be taken full or part time. The university also offers a BSc in Psychology with Neuroscience and a BSc in Cognitive Sciences. All three degrees are accredited by the BPS as conferring eligibility for graduate membership with GBC.

WINCHESTER

The University of Winchester
West Hill
Winchester, SO22 4NR
Tel: 01962 827302
www.winchester.ac.uk/?page=3033

The Department of Psychology has an excellent track record in teaching and research. In 2009, the *Guardian Good University Guide* ranked the quality of teaching as the 5th best in the UK. The BSc Psychology is offered as a Single Honours programme, though students may choose a Combined honours programme in which psychology is studied either as a major, joint or minor subject. The Single Honours programme is accredited by the BPS, and confers eligibility for the GBC, provided the minimum standard of qualification of Second Class Honours is achieved. This is the first step to becoming a chartered psychologist. Students study all the major sub-disciplines of psychology and conduct a range of hands-on practical work. In the final year, students pursue an in-depth research project, and take courses relating to applied areas of psychology, as well as the department's research strengths in cognitive, developmental and social psychology. The Department of Psychology also has good regional, national and international links, including a number of Erasmus exchange opportunities.

WOLVERHAMPTON

The University of Wolverhampton
Wulfruna Street
Wolverhampton WV1 1SB
Tel: 01902 321000
www.wlv.ac.uk/science/psychology

Wolverhampton offers three-year degree courses, all accredited by the BPS as conferring eligibility for graduate membership with GBC. These courses cover the core areas within the BPS curriculum whilst allowing students to develop areas of personal interest, and enabling them to develop their skills as independent learners and critical thinkers. All courses are available full time or part time.

The following courses are available:

- BSc Hons Psychology
- BSc Hons Psychology in Combined Awards
- BSc Hons Counselling Psychology.

WORCESTER

University of Worcester
Henwick Grove
Worcester WR2 6AJ
Tel: 01905 855000
www.worc.ac.uk/psychology

Students may follow a Single Honours, major, joint or minor pathway in psychology. The Single Honours and major pathways are accredited by the BPS as conferring eligibility for graduate membership with GBC, provided that the specified route is followed. Psychology combines well with health studies, business management, biological science, sociology and education studies. The department has specific research interests in the areas of health psychology, occupational psychology, developmental psychology and cognitive psychology. It also runs a number of taught master's level courses: the MSc Issues in Applied Psychology, which offers specific pathway options in abnormal and clinical, business and developmental psychology; and an MSc in Occupational/Organisational Psychology. A Postgraduate Certificate in Changing Health Behaviours is also run, as is a conversion course – the Graduate Diploma in Psychology. Psychology also offers master's and Doctoral level degrees by research, and each year there are a number of PhD studentships available through competition.

YORK

The University of York
Heslington
York YO10 5DD
Tel: 01904 430000
www.york.ac.uk/depts/psych

York's BSc (Hons) Psychology degree offers an overall coverage of the subject with particular emphasis on psychology as an experimental science and academic discipline. After studying all major areas of psychology in the first two years, students in the final year choose from a range of advanced modules, and complete a literature survey and a project. The programme is accredited by the BPS as conferring eligibility for graduate membership with GBC. The Department of Psychology has consistently received the highest ratings for teaching and research.

YORK ST JOHN

York St John University
Lord Mayor's Walk
York YO31 7EX
Tel: 01904 624624
www.yorksj.ac.uk

Psychology is available as either a BSc Single Honours degree, a BA Single Honours degree or a BA Joint Honours degree, on a full- or part-time basis. The BSc Honours degree is accredited by the BPS as conferring eligibility the GBC. The BA Single Honours and Joint Honours degrees do not confer GBC. The programmes provide a sound core knowledge of psychology and how it applies to different aspects of the human condition, such as crime, mental health, child development or education. The BA Honours degree deliberately deviates from the BPS syllabus, placing less emphasis on statistics and biology and more on applications of psychology. All tutors have backgrounds in research and applied psychology. A one-year Graduate Diploma conversion course is also available, as are postgraduate degrees by research. The Graduate Diploma allows graduates who have studied some non-accredited psychology in their first degree to obtain the GBC through extra study and is accredited by the BPS.

■ BPS ACCREDIATION

As outlined in Chapter 1, the BPS accredits certain psychology courses, meaning that graduates of these courses are eligible to apply for graduate membership of the BPS and for the GBC, which is required for the pursuit of professional training in psychology and is often referred to as the first step towards becoming a chartered psychologist. The table below provides a quick reference for checking which institutions run BPS-accredited psychology courses. More detailed information is given on pages 45–97 but do check the institutions' websites too. Note that eligibility to apply for the GBC is often subject to achieving at least a Second Class Honours degree on BPS-accredited courses.

Universities offering BPS accredited courses

ABERDEEN	YES	CARDIFF	YES
ABERTAY DUNDEE	YES	CHESTER	YES
ANGLIA RUSKIN	YES	CITY	YES
ASTON	YES	COVENTRY	YES
BANGOR	YES	DE MONTFORT	YES
BATH	YES	DERBY	YES
BATH SPA	YES	DUNDEE	YES
BEDFORDSHIRE	YES	DURHAM	YES
BIRMINGHAM	YES	EAST LONDON	YES
BOLTON	YES	EDGE HILL	YES
BOURNEMOUTH	YES	EDINBURGH	YES
BRADFORD	YES	EDINBURGH NAPIER	YES
BRISTOL	YES	ESSEX	YES
BRISTOL UWE	YES	EXETER	YES
BRUNEL	YES	GLAMORGAN	YES
BUCKINGHAM	NO	GLASGOW	YES
BUCKINGHAMSHIRE NEW	YES	GLASGOW CALEDONIAN	YES
CAMBRIDGE	YES	GLOUCESTERSHIRE	YES
CANTERBURY CHRIST CHURCH	YES	GOLDSMITHS	YES

(Continued)

GREENWICH	YES	QUEEN MARGARET	YES
HERTFORDSHIRE	YES	QUEEN'S BELFAST	YES
HUDDERSFIELD	YES	READING	YES
HULL	YES	ROEHAMPTON	YES
KEELE	YES	ROYAL HOLLOWAY	YES
KENT	YES	ST ANDREWS	YES
KINGSTON	YES	SHEFFIELD	YES
LANCASTER	YES	SHEFFIELD HALLAM	YES
LEEDS	YES	SOUTHAMPTON	YES
LEEDS TRINITY	YES	SOUTHAMPTON SOLENT	NO
LEICESTER	YES	STAFFORDSHIRE	YES
LINCOLN	YES	STIRLING	YES
LIVERPOOL	YES	STRATHCLYDE	YES
LIVERPOOL HOPE	YES	SUNDERLAND	YES
LIVERPOOL JOHN MOORES	YES	SURREY	YES
LONDON METROPOLITAN	YES	SUSSEX	YES
LONDON SOUTH BANK	YE	SWANSEA	YES
LOUGHBOROUGH	YES	TEESSIDE	YES
LUTON	YES	THAMES VALLEY	YES
MANCHESTER	YES	UCL	YES
MANCHESTER MET	YES	UCLan	YES
MIDDLESEX	YES	ULSTER	YES
MMU CHESHIRE	NO	UWIC	YES
NEWCASTLE	YES	WARWICK	YES
NORTHAMPTON	YES	WEST OF SCOTLAND	YES
NORTHUMBRIA	YES	WESTMINSTER	YES
NOTTINGHAM	YES	WINCHESTER	YES
NOTTINGHAM TRENT	YES	WOLVERHAMPTON	YES
OXFORD	YES	WORCESTER	YES
OXFORD BROOKES	YES	YORK	YES
PLYMOUTH	YES	YORK ST JOHN	YES
PORTSMOUTH	YES		

Not all courses offered at these institutions will lead to BPS; please see individual university entries for details.

08 Further information

British Psychological Society

The British Psychological Society (BPS) is the professional association for psychologists and is incorporated by Royal Charter. A Register of Chartered Psychologists was established in 1987, bringing a more organised and stricter discipline to the profession. Chartered psychologists are bound to an ethical code of conduct which was set up to maintain the standards of psychology as a profession and to protect the public. The Society publishes a useful pamphlet, 'So you want to be a Psychologist' – essential reading for prospective psychologists – and a range of information leaflets. The Register lists members of the Society who have reached a certain standard in education and work experience. It contains their names, qualifications and work addresses. Copies of the Register can be found at main public reference libraries and at professional organisations and certain employer bodies. The Register is split into specialist areas such as clinical, criminological and legal, educational, occupational and counselling psychology.

To qualify for registration as a chartered psychologist you must:

- have completed a first qualification in psychology that is a GBC
- have undergone a further course or supervised training in a specific area of psychology
- have agreed to abide by a Code of Conduct laid down by the BPS
- be judged fit to practise psychology without supervision.

For further information contact:

The British Psychological Society
St Andrews House
48 Princess Road East
Leicester LE1 7DR
www.bps.org.uk

The British Association of Sport and Exercise Sciences (BASES)
Leeds Metropolitan University
Carnegie Faculty of Sport and Education
Fairfax Hall
Headingley Campus
Beckett Park
Leeds LS6 3QS
www.bases.org.uk

UK Council for Psychotherapy
2nd Floor
Edward House
2 Wakley Street
London EC1V 7LT
Tel: 020 7436 3002
www.psychotherapy.org.uk

The Association of Educational Psychologists
26 The Avenue
Durham DH1 4ED
www.aep.org.uk

The British Association for Counselling and Psychotherapy
35–37 Albert Street
Rugby CV21 2SG
www.bacp.co.uk

General university guides

Degree Course Offers, Brian Heap, published annually by Trotman Publishing, www.trotman.co.uk

Entrance Guide to Higher Education in Scotland, published by UCAS, PO Box 28, Cheltenham, Gloucestershire GE52 3LZ, www.ucas.com

Guide to UK Universities 2010, Klaus Boehm and Jenny Lees-Spalding (eds), published by Trotman Publishing, www.trotman.co.uk

Guide to Student Money, Gwenda Thomas, published annually by Trotman Publishing, www.trotman.co.uk

How to Complete Your UCAS Application, published annually by Trotman Publishing, www.trotman.co.uk

How to Write a Winning UCAS Personal Statement, Ian Stannard, Trotman Publishing, www.trotman.co.uk

The UCAS Handbook is free to UK addresses from UCAS, PO Box 28, Cheltenham, Gloucestershire GL52 3LZ, www.ucas.com

University and College Entrance: The Official Guide, published by UCAS (see above)

University Scholarships, Awards & Bursaries, Brian Heap, published by Trotman Publishing, www.trotman.co.uk

Which Uni? Find the Best University for You, Karla Fitzhugh, Trotman Publishing, www.trotman.co.uk

Psychology texts

As far as specific psychology textbooks go, any of the introductory texts found in large bookshops are fine. Those relating to social psychology are probably the easiest and most interesting to read if you are new to the subject.

A User's Guide to the Brain, John Ratey, Abacus

Body Language, Allan Pease, Sheldon Press

Dictionary of Psychology, Andrew M Colman, Cambridge University Press

Emotional Intelligence, Daniel Goleman, Bloomsbury

From the Edge of the Couch, Raj Persaud, Bantam

Introduction in Psychology, Atkinson and Hilgard, Wadsworth

Mapping the Mind, Rita Carter, Weidenfeld & Nicolson

Memory, David Samuel, Phoenix

The Moral Animal – The New Science of Evolutionary Psychology, Robert Wright, Abacus

The Noonday Demon – An Anatomy of Depression, Andrew Solomon, Chatto & Windus

Penguin Dictionary of Psychology, Reber and Reber, Penguin

Phobias – Fighting the Fear, Helen Saul, HarperCollins

QI – The Quest for Intelligence, Kevin Warwick, Piatkus

The Human Mind, Robert Winston, Bantam

Tomorrow's People, Susan Greenfield, Penguin

Totem and Talent, Sigmund Freud, Routledge

Psychologies (Magazine available from newsagents)

Websites

Business Psychology News: www.businesspsychologist.com
British Psychological Society: www.bps.org.uk
Psych Central: www.psychcentral.com
Psychology Today: www.psychologytoday.com

Choose the right qualifications